④⓪ Days
and
④⓪ Bytes

Making Computers Work for Your Congregation

Aaron Spiegel, Nancy Armstrong, and Brent Bill

THE
ALBAN
INSTITUTE

Herndon, Virginia
www.alban.org

First Rowman & Littlefield paperback edition 2014

Published by Rowman & Littlefield
4501 Forbes Blvd, Suite 200, Lanham, MD 20706
www.rowman.com

10 Thornbury Road, Plymouth PL6 7PP, United Kingdom

Unless otherwise indicated, scripture quotations are from the New Revised Standard Version of the Bible © 1989, Division of Christian Education of the National Council of Churches of Christ in the United States of America, and are used by permission.

Library of Congress Cataloging-in-Publication Data Available

Spiegel, Aaron, 1961-
    40 days and 40 bytes : making computers work for your congregation / by Aaron Spiegel, Nancy Armstrong, and Brent Bill.
       p. cm.
    ISBN 978-1-56699-298-5
    1. Church work--Data processing. I. Title: Forty days and forty bytes. II. Armstrong, Nancy, 1957- III. Bill, J. Brent, 1951- IV. Title.

    BV652.77.S66 2004
    254'.00285--dc22
                                    2004008566

Ⓧ™ The paper used in this publication meets the minimum requirements of American National Standard for Information Sciences

Printed in the United States of America

Cover design by Adele Robey, Phoenix Graphics

Contents

Preface

"Excuse me."

"Is that you again, Moses?"

"I'm afraid it is."

"More computer problems?"

"How did you guess?"

"I don't have to guess."

"Ah. I forgot."

"Tell me what you want, Moses."

"I thought you already knew?"

"Moses!"

"Sorry."

"Well, go ahead. Spit it out."

"Well, I have a question. You know those ten 'things' you e-mailed me?"

"The Ten Commandments."

"That's it. I was wondering . . . are they important?"

"What do you mean 'important'? Of course, they're important. Otherwise, I wouldn't have sent them to you."

"Well, I lost them. Sorry. I could say the dog ate them, but of course you'd see right through that."

"What do you mean you 'lost them'? You didn't save them?"

"I forgot."

"Always save, Moses."

"Yes, I know, you've told me that before. But I did forward them to some people before I lost them."

"And did you hear back from any of them?"

"You already know I did. There was one guy who said he never uses 'shalt not.' May he change the words a little bit?"

"Yes, Moses, but he shalt not change the meaning."

"And there's a guy who thought your stance was a little harsh, and recommended calling them the 'Ten Suggestions,' or letting people pick one or two to try for a while."

"Moses, I will pretend I did not hear that."

"And I'll take that as a 'no.' Well, what about the guy who said I was scamming him?"

"Spamming."

"Right! I e-mailed him back and told him I can't even eat that stuff, and I have no idea how you can send meat to someone through a computer."

"And what did he say?"

"Oh, I can't repeat it. He used Your name in vain."

"Hmm."

"You don't think he might have sent me one of those—err—'plagues,' and that's the reason I lost those ten 'things,' do you?"

"They're called 'viruses.' You think just anyone can send a plague?"

"Ugh! This computer stuff is just too much for me. Can we go back to using stone tablets? Kinda hard to carry around, but at least I never lost them."

"No, Moses. We will do it the new way, using computers!"

"I was afraid you'd say that."

"Moses, what did I tell you to do if you messed up?"

"You told me to hold up this rat and point it toward the computer."

"It's a mouse, Moses, not a rat. Mouse! Mouse! And did you do that?"

"No, I decided to try calling technical support first. After all, who knows more about this stuff than you? And I like your hours. By the way, did Noah have two of these mice on the ark?"

"No, Moses."

"One other thing. Why didn't you name them 'frogs' instead of 'mice'—since they sit on a pad?"

"I did not name them, Moses. Man did, and you can call yours a frog if you want to."

"Oh, that explains it. I bet some woman told Adam to call it a mouse. After all, wasn't it a woman who named one of the computers an 'Apple?'"

"Say good night, Moses."

"Oh, Look! I am pointing the mouse, and it seems to be working. Yes, a couple of the ten 'things' have come back."

"Which ones are they, Moses?"

"Let me see. 'Thou shalt not steal from any grave an image' and 'Thou shalt not uncover Thy neighbor's wife.'"

"Turn the computer off, Moses. I'm sending you another set of stone tablets."

THE MICROCHIP CHURCH*
William H. Willimon

There was this boy in my class in high school. He was the most out-of-it person I knew. He wore shoes with laces, white shirts and white socks, and used Vitalis. He was always talking about how interesting some algebra problem was on last night's homework.

You can imagine my surprise on meeting this fellow at a high-school reunion and learning that he now lives in California overlooking the beach—one of those exclusive places where everyone is into consciousness-raising and owns a Doberman. He came to the reunion with a beard and blue jeans and driving a Rolls. It turns out that this guy has invented a computer game. He thought it up one night while watching "Family Feud." He programmed the game that night after the show, set up his own company the next morning, and had already sold over $2 million worth of stock before dinner that evening. By the next day the stock had divided twice; needless to say, he is now very, very well off. I haven't actually seen the game, but it is something about a family of gnomes who are trying to find the Holy Grail through a maze of monsters.

He is now working on a game he wouldn't say much about, in which the gnomes set up a theme amusement park after they find the Grail. The computer takes them through the adventures of setting up their own corporation. Atari is said to be positively frantic over the prospect.

So I went home from the high-school reunion depressed as the devil. "That could have been *me,*" I thought.

Why him? Sure, I was never too good in algebra, but I've always had a storehouse of good ideas. Look at me, 38, living in a Methodist parsonage and driving a Dart. Look who's Mr. Out-of-It now. There is the fabulous, brave new world of computers and here is the church. There is Columbus launching out into unexplored territory and here I am, staying home, perfecting the Gregorian chant.

But that was yesterday. You've heard of the electronic church. Well, I now serve the first microchip church. While other pastors are sipping coffee at Ministerial Association meetings and visiting nursing homes, I have been quietly putting together a computerized ministry conglomerate. Friends ask, "How do you do it?" It's a simple blend of economic savvy and good old American ingenuity.

It is somewhat odd that I should be presiding over a multimillion-dollar church. In seminary, nobody thought that I showed much promise

---

for ministry. One of my professors told me after I took his liturgics exam that I ought to consider using my talents in real estate rather than in administering the Eucharist.

My entry into the new age of computers began when I contemplated leading the upcoming fall Bible study group, a job I've always detested. As always, it was going to be on Paul. I thought of all those long hours in the church parlor getting more and more depressed at the idea. Then it occurred to me: Why not devise a game to do it for me—a "Pac-Man" for Paul?

I took a crash course in programming at our local Radio Shack. In two weeks, I had what is, as far as I know, the first computerized Bible action game. Using a little stick and a television screen, the computer takes a tiny Paul on his journey through Asia Minor. Jail, beatings, thorns in the flesh, Judaizers, the circumcision party—they're all there. The player has to figure out how Paul is going to make it to his heavenly reward in Rome.

The United Methodist Bible study group loved it. They would never go back to the old way of Bible study. The church parlor, which used to be adorned with large wing chairs, two sofas and a Sallman's *Head of Christ,* is now this country's first Christian video arcade. I have since added a number of neat games such as "Samson and the Philistines" and "Ten Difficult Sayings of Jesus Made Easy." Needless to say, the kids love it. How many churches do you know that have to run the teenagers out of the church in the evening in order to lock up?

We are now negotiating with a number of denominational publishing houses to market our line of Bible-based video games, although Sears may be our best prospect. I predict that in four or five years the familiar Sunday-school quarterly will be as antiquated as a Temperance Society pledge card is today and my church, thanks to royalties and residuals from our software, will make the income of the Crystal Cathedral look like that of the little church in the wildwood.

Things went so well with our first foray into the world of computers that we decided to computerize everything in the church. We bought a new IBM system with terminals in all the church offices. As a means of pastoral care, the computer is virtually limitless. Everybody in my church is now on our computer, with their complete personal information and record of giving. At the punch of a button we can send everyone a birthday card, anniversary card, recognition of any personal event in their lives, or a reminder of how far behind they are on their pledge. Every day our computer pulls people's names and makes a personal call to them (using a recording of my voice) which goes something like this: "Hello, [name inserted]. This is your pastor. Just wanted you to know that I was thinking about you in my prayer time this morning. Isn't this the day you married [or divorced, were robbed, graduated, got certified, were promoted, or fired, or 200 other categories of human experience] last year? Why, certainly I remembered. How could I forget? Good-bye, (X)."

How many traditionalist pastors do you know who can do this?

Our computer is now our number-one evangelism aid. We have an on-line connection with the local police station, family court, credit bureau, and electric company. We receive a printout each day of every-one who moves into town, everyone who is arrested, all filings for di-vorce and child custody, and upcoming cases in civil court. Talk about matching the gospel to human need! Imagine the impression we make on a family who has just had the lights turned off for nonpayment of their electric bill when a church team shows up offering to have prayer with them. A year ago, we couldn't have done that.

We also utilize our electronic genius for more activist concerns. Within minutes I can send personal letters to every congressperson in our state's delegation, each letter signed by a member of our congrega-tion, protesting some pending legislation. Can you imagine the impact on a politician of receiving a thousand letters in a day expressing righ-teous indignation over his vote yesterday?

When the bishop tried to move me last year because of the com-plaints of a group of malcontents in the congregation—conservative Neanderthals who don't know a cathode-ray tube from a concordance—guess who got a thousand personal letters expressing shock and dis-may? We are also able to send personalized sympathy cards and get-well cards to any district superintendent in our conference. Some people sit around and wait for the Holy Spirit to work; I prefer to peck out new programs that make a few things happen when they ought to.

While other pastors are pounding the pavement, knocking on doors, beating out sermons, I have just sent letters to every charismatic fe-male over the age of 35 with a college degree who owns her own home and has an income of over $30,000 a year, to tell each one personally about our special upcoming Labor Day service. I am writing this article on my word processor, which automatically filters out bad spelling, in-correct grammar, and homiletical clichés at the touch of a button.

Think of what Martin Luther could have done with this technology!

When Will Willimon wrote this piece 20 years ago, it was pretty easy to take it as farce—a satirical look at the emerging strange new world of com-puters. "How silly," many laughed. "That could never happen." And yet, as we now know, his piece was less satiric than it was prophetic. Today we are awash in computerized Bible games, pastoral-care software, and church management systems that track members' personal information and giving records. As Willimon cynically predicted, at the punch of a button, churches and synagogues can send birthday cards, anniversary cards, and recognition of personal events—as well as reminders of how far behind members are on their pledges. Phone trees enable congregations to make "personal calls" to members. Everything Willimon had us smirking at has happened. Technology is so much a part of contemporary congregational culture that nobody raises an eyebrow about it anymore.

This widespread computer use is both good and bad. It's good, because people of faith need to adapt technology to their ministry needs. We have a long history of having done so. First it was recording oral traditions on papyrus with ink. Then it was on to the printing press. Next came typewriters. Today it's computers, PDAs, and cell phones

But this pervasive use of technology can also be bad—often because we blindly accept and use it without asking the big questions. Questions such as, "Is it appropriate to our mission and ministry?" or "Just because it's available, or because First Megachurch uses it, does that mean we should?"

And that's one of the best things about Willimon's piece. It reminds us of those questions. Helping your congregation find your answer to those questions is this book's purpose. We're going to help your congregation explore technology and its tools. That way you can decide, from a ministry and cultural standpoint, what you need to do.

We're uniquely qualified to assist you in looking at these questions and thinking about the role of technology in your congregation. That's because, since its inception in 1997, the Indianapolis Center for Congregations has worked with over 400 congregations around the issue of congregations and technology. We have helped congregations with technology-related topics such as finding and funding hardware, Internet usage, congregation management software (CMS), and much more. As part of its work, in 1998 the Center began its innovative Computers and Ministry Grants Initiative (CMGI). This program was designed to help congregations address the challenges in using computer technology for important ministries to their members and constituencies. CMGI worked with 102 congregations. It awarded almost 2 million dollars in matching grants for hardware, software, training, service, and support.

We were faced with a dilemma in February 1998 when the Center created the "Computers and Ministry" courses. Our primary goal was to give a broad background of what was available in the area of technology for congregations. We weren't going to train congregations on the specifics of any hardware or software; we assumed that someone somewhere had created a program like that. We were wrong. We had to design it ourselves—so we did.

Aaron and Nancy were the two primary developers of CMGI. They did so based on their expertise in technology and congregations. That expertise continues today.

Aaron's work for the Center includes resource consulting with area congregations on better use of technology in enhancing congregational effectiveness and efficiency. He also manages the Center's in-house technology systems and various database and information systems projects. Since 1983, he has operated ARS Productions, a consulting firm specializing in technology solutions for congregations, nonprofit institutions, and businesses. A transdenominational rabbi, Aaron holds rabbinic ordination from both Rabbinical Seminary International and The Rabbinical Academy of Mesifta Adas Wolkowisk.

Nancy is the Center's finance director. She's a former church administrator who specializes in the area of computer technology. She has served as a business administrator and consultant to several Indianapolis congregations. Just before coming to the Indianapolis Center for Congregations, Nancy was Director of Finance and Computer Services at St. Luke's United Methodist Church in Indianapolis, one of the largest United Methodist churches in the Midwest.

Unlike Aaron and Nancy, Brent isn't a computer expert. He does know how to log on every morning. That's it. He's just a technology user. But as the Center's executive vice president and the person responsible for communicating what we're learning, he has sat through many of the CMGI classes and reunions. In doing so, he's heard how technology has made a difference, both good and bad, in congregational life. He is a writer, too. And so he, as a nontechie, is translating what Aaron and Nancy have learned into plain language.

In this book we're going to use what we have learned to help you explore how your congregation can use technology. We're not going teach you how to develop software or use technology so that, like Willimon's fictional pastor, you can bring in so much money that it'll "make the income of the Crystal Cathedral look like that of the little church in the wildwood." It's not our goal to turn you into "The Microchip Church—or Synagogue." We will help you design technology uses that fit with your ministry and mission. Our goal is Godly service—not technological glitz. Still, it's obvious that there's no question that your congregation is going to use computer technology. The only question is "how?".

Let's take a look at how some congregations have answered that question.

Acknowledgments

The Computers and Ministry Grants Initiative (CMGI), the program that led to this book, was a team project. Aaron was the team leader and Nancy helped him cocreate it. As the organizers and managers of the project, it was their pleasure to work with a group of dedicated, passionate, capable professionals who united for a common purpose—to help congregations use technology as a part of their ministry. We acknowledge and thank them.

First, our consultants. These folks worked directly with congregations. They took the information from the class sessions and helped make it specific and applicable to each congregation. It was hard finding people who had the unique combined skill sets of experience with congregations and technology, but these people did it well. They are Sue Weber, Denise Smith, Steve Clark, Brigitte Black, Molly Ellsworth, and Susan Sveen.

Of course, without the support of our colleagues at the Indianapolis Center for Congregations, the program and ensuing book would not have been possible. This project consumed a great deal of the Center's resources for more than three years. It could not have been as successful without the generosity of time and spirit from the Center staff. We particularly thank Janice Phillips and Jerri Kinder for their fabulous administrative support and Nancy DeMott who was instrumental in creating the original curriculum. Tim Shapiro, the Center's president, could always be counted on to drop by and offer words of support for "our" book.

We also need to thank John Wimmer and the Lilly Endowment. John, the Indianapolis Center's founding director, was a tireless champion of this program. He made sure the Endowment knew that we were really touching people's lives. Lilly Endowment Inc. made it all possible by generously funding the work.

We also acknowledge, with gratitude, the support of our Alban publishing colleagues. Beth Ann Gaede and Rochelle Melander especially helped with kind, wise, and firm editorial guidance and suggestions.

In addition to our combined acknowledgments, we each have some special people we want to recognize.

Aaron acknowledges "his wonderful wife Kelly and three amazing children, Hannah, Elijah, and Gabriel. Without their support and commitment to my passion the CMGI program would not have succeeded."

Nancy thanks "Diane Brown and Velma Buck, extraordinary women and dedicated teachers. They contributed more to my life than they will ever know. Thanks also go to my daughter Jenna, whose delightful spirit and quick wit provided welcome relief when writing became a chore. And to my husband Kevin, friend and life partner, whose love and encouragement make all the difference every day."

Brent says, "thanks for your support in this book project, and life, to Nancy [Bill]. You have supported my writing and computer habits for many years. I guess that makes you a co-computer-dependent. Nancy, now that this book is finally finished, I promise I will not retreat upstairs to my computer right after dinner. But then I make that promise every time I finish a book, don't I?"

Finally, the three of us acknowledge—us. We had a great time planning and writing this book together. It was a lot of work, but each of us contributed her or his part with grace, care, and lots of laughter. Let's not do it again real soon.

We need to say one more thing. That is that everyone involved in this project worked selflessly, tirelessly, and without complaint for the betterment of congregations. Their time and participation were a blessing. Aaron's tradition teaches *mitokh shelo lishmah, ba lishmah*—that people do things without ulterior motive, without the intention to please God, but because those actions are the right thing to do and their minds and hearts are set to the right purpose. This describes the Computers and Ministry team.

Aaron Spiegel, Nancy Armstrong, and Brent Bill
Indianapolis 2004

A Tale of Two Congregations— and Technology

> It was the best of times, it was the worst of times, it was the age of wisdom, it was the age of foolishness, it was the epoch of belief, it was the epoch of incredulity, . . . it was the spring of hope, it was the winter of despair, we had everything before us, we had nothing before us . . . —in short, the period was so far like the present period.
> —Charles Dickens, *A Tale of Two Cities*

Was Dickens writing about computers and congregations? Of course not, but his words resonate with us. Congregations working with computers have had the best of times and the worst of times. They have been wise— and foolish. Some believed that computers could solve their problems— and then were incredulous that they have not. They unwrapped boxes of software with a spirit of hope, and then were covered in a winter of despair when something went wrong that they could not figure out. They have had everything before them—and then a blank monitor screen of nothing before them.

We want to make your use of technology the best of times, an age of wisdom, an epoch of belief, to fill you with the spirit of hope, and place the best of everything before you. Okay, maybe that is overstating it a bit. But we do want to guide you through the amazing maze of congregations and technology and help you come out in the best of times at the other end. So let's start with the tale of two congregations.*

PEACEFUL GROVE PRESBYTERIAN CHURCH

Remember the old hymn lyric, "the little brown church in the vale"? That is an accurate description of the Peaceful Grove Presbyterian Church. When

---

* The names of these two congregations have been changed to protect the computer innocents.

we begin their story, this small rural congregation had just celebrated its 150th anniversary. It had been a year of change for them and their surroundings. The large farm across the road was being divided into lots for 200 new homes. Their country community was changing into a suburb. Although the church members valued their small, close-knit worshiping community, they felt called to respond to changes around them. They formed a visioning team. The team was charged with charting the course for building on congregational strengths and expanding ministries to meet the new needs.

Part of the team's work involved building the church's capacity to support their new vision. Technology was one of the areas needing more capacity. Peaceful Grove owned one old computer and inkjet printer. Both were in the pastor's office. The pastor and the church secretary shared this equipment. They used it for everything—word processing, keeping the membership list and mailing label list, and their limited connection to the Internet. Meanwhile, the treasurer used her own home computer for financial record keeping. They recorded contributions by hand.

The congregation realized that technology held great potential and they wanted to take advantage of that potential as they grew. So they formed a computer technology team to analyze their immediate and long-range computer needs. Some team members were exceptionally tech-savvy. Others knew little about technology, but did know a lot about the congregation and its ministry. Working together, the team identified several areas where computer technology could be useful to their church. Then they created a needs list for each area of church work. Next they converted those lists into detailed plans. Finally, the team began implementing them.

It was not always easy. Sometimes team members had different points of view. Money was not immediately available to accommodate everyone's wish list. Bad weather and less-than-perfect service technicians also complicated their process. But in the end they accomplished a great deal.

Peaceful Grove ended up purchasing two desktop computers, one notebook computer, and creating a small network. They decided to buy an inexpensive, but well-written, church management software program and a widely used small-business accounting program. Their tech team enjoyed a Saturday night spending spree at a local electronics store. There they bought a scanner, the notebook computer, a digital camera, and a digital camcorder. They ordered a small multimedia projector. They began working on a church Web site. One year later they converted a classroom into a small media center, purchased three more computers, and loaded them with educational and Bible study software.

Because of the technology team's work, this church is better prepared to face its exciting future. Their church management and accounting software helped eliminate and streamline much record keeping. The church staff communicates more easily to the congregation via mailings and e-mails. The additional office computers lowered frustration and increased efficiency among the staff. The projector enhances the worship experience in many ways, including a means to highlight and say thank you to worship volunteers. It is also used for mission trip presentations.

Using their digital camera and camcorder, Peaceful Grove members have recorded many congregational activities. These include new members classes, confirmation activities, pancake breakfasts, the installation of a new steeple, and Bible school. Slide shows of these activities are presented during the Sunday coffee hour. Everyone gathers around to see who and what will show up each week.

The church has also begun taping worship services for homebound members. The confirmation class recently used the media center to research possible mission projects. The church's Web site, still in its beginning, has generated a lot of excitement among the members. They plan to purchase a large banner featuring their Web site address. It will be placed in the church's front yard for those who drive by each day to see—especially those folks in the 200 new homes across the road.

When asked about the impact of this project on their congregation, the pastor said that the increased technology helped raise the awareness of other mission and outreach opportunities available to the congregation. It engaged the youth more in the life of their church. Computers and software helped the pastor and secretary be more efficient administratively—and reduced their frustration levels. Better and timelier communications are being sent to the congregation. And when the church was making plans for a new fellowship hall, they had the foresight to think about how technology would be incorporated into the new building—for ministry's sake.

As they move into the future, Peaceful Grove Church realizes that technology has become, and will remain, a ministry of the congregation. Their long-term plans—focusing on church growth and outreach—include a technology component. Computer technology found a home at Peaceful Grove.

ST. JAMES CHURCH

St. James Church is located on one of this capitol city's most prestigious streets. Its sprawling campus of beautiful stone buildings and carefully tended green spaces present the perfect picture of a large church. The congregation enjoys a long history in the community. It is known as the church home of many wealthy city leaders. When this congregation built or bought something, it was first class all the way.

One example of this first-class thinking was the purchase of a state-of-the-art computer network and the latest, and most expensive, church database software. It was expensive, but St. James thought a church of its size needed that kind of technology. Surprisingly, some board members were concerned about cost. That was solved when a computer programmer in the congregation volunteered to take care of all this new equipment and provide software support. It was his gift to the church. This gift saved a great deal of money.

They also saved money, they thought, by cutting training. Since database work was viewed as "administrative," it was felt that only two people in the church office needed training on the new congregation management software. Likewise, since the equipment was so new, no one saw a need to include computer maintenance funds in the annual budget for a couple of years. That also saved money—or seemed to.

Over the next few years, the volunteer wearied from receiving so many technology help calls from the church. He honored his commitment the best that he could, but increased work responsibilities meant that there were times he could not respond to the church's needs until the following week. The church staff was frustrated with all the computer problems that took a long time to fix. But what could they say? The volunteer tried his best, his services were free, and he was a congregational leader.

Then both administrative staff members left the church. When they left, each had brief opportunities to show their replacements how they had used the computer. Still, the new staff received no formal training.

One of the new staff members had experimented with setting up small-group codes and committee rosters. That never worked well and no one asked him for that kind of information anyway. And the expensive membership database? Well, it was mainly used just to create mailing labels and to send contribution statements.

When they first installed their computer network, it included a staff e-mail system. It worked fine—at first. But since there were frequent network problems that disabled the e-mail (and took a long time to get fixed), the staff found that telephone calls and handwritten notes were their most reliable means of communication.

One day the vendor of St. James's congregation management software called. He announced that the company was ending its support for the version of the software that St. James used. It was too old. Most of their customers had upgraded to newer versions; however, St. James had not. The vendor offered the church a special price if the church converted now. Eager to take advantage of this offer, they quickly ordered the software. When it arrived, the new staff member who took care of the computers (in addition to her regular administrative duties) noticed that the minimum computer hardware requirements for this version far exceeded those of most of St. James's computer workstations.

Their network was old, their workstations were old, their operating software was old, and no one had noticed until then. There was no money in the budget for that fiscal year—and the year had just begun.

WHY COMPUTERS AND CONGREGATIONS?

The above are the best of stories, and the worst of stories. Stories like these are one reason that in January 1998 the Indianapolis Center for Congregations embarked on its ambitious project of teaching congregations how to use technology to enhance congregational ministry. Our main goal was to provide a broad background of what was available for congregations technologically. We did not have a particular implied or explicit theology—we wanted congregations to think practically and theologically about computer use. That included all aspects of using technology in congregations—desktop publishing, member records, accounting, word processing, communications, the Internet, presentations, education, and so on. As we said in the preface, it was not our goal to train congregations on the specifics of any hardware or software. We were not offering classes on using Word or PowerPoint.

Since nobody had created the kind of program we envisioned, that left it up to us. We began an intensive three-month process of interviewing congregations, researching trends, and creating a curriculum. Our interviews centered around our desire to create awareness of "what's out there" for congregations and then teach them how to go about accessing the services, hardware, software, and training necessary to implement new or updated technology in their congregations.

The result was "Computers and Ministry: Making Technology Work for Your Congregation." Designed as a series of three all-day workshops, we also planned on including some on-site consulting visits. This workshop series soon evolved into a grants program called the "Computers and Ministry Grants Initiative" (CMGI), which we mentioned in the preface.

That is because we realized that teaching congregations about what they could do with technology and how it can ultimately aid the life of congregants, and then not providing them with the financial resources to implement technology, seemed cruel. Our ability to shift from pure teaching about computers and ministry to making grants for it came about due to the Lilly Endowment Inc. and its interest and generosity.

Also, we felt that that instituting a grants program along with the training would make us the recipients of a wealth of information about how congregations use (and misuse) technology. We could see what worked—and what didn't. We were right. What we learned forms the basis for much of what follows.

The Indianapolis Center for Congregations continues to work with congregations in the area of technology. This work has grown out of our experience with CMGI and our ongoing effort to provide up-to-date information on the state of technology and its possible implications for churches, synagogues, and mosques. The calls keep coming.

ERROR MESSAGES

One important thing we tell congregations is that there is a great deal of misinformation about congregational technology. Salespeople sometimes lead congregations in directions that are not helpful. Since one of our roles as resource consultants is to help Indianapolis area congregations assess and understand proposals from vendors, we are often present during sales pitches. The old joke, "How do you know when a computer salesman is lying?—His lips are moving," is not exactly true. We have found, however, that not all salespeople represent their products and services correctly. Many times that is because as salespeople and not day-to-day users or techies, they do not adequately understand the underlying technology of their own products. Other times it's because they do not comprehend congregational culture. Most salespeople are used to working with businesses. And while every congregation has aspects of business to it, rarely does a congregation operate like a business. That is not surprising, since its purpose is so different.

We, unlike hardware or software salespeople, are not trying to sell you anything. Our goal is to provide you with a clear picture of what technology can do for your congregation—all from a perspective that you know what you want and need to do better than any salesperson. Our objective is to help you help yourself.

Another thing we learned is that one of our tasks is often to convince computer nonusers (usually pastors or rabbis) that they use computers all the time. It is nearly impossible not to. We use a computer every time we telephone (whether cellular or not), withdraw money from an ATM, or start our car. All of these devices are controlled, in large part, by computers. Granted, these computers are single- or limited-function devices. But they are computers nonetheless. Like it or not, everyone uses a computer. So next time one of these nonbelievers says, "I'll never use a computer," you can unequivocally tell them they are wrong!

So now you know our qualifications. You have also heard some best of—and worst of—stories from congregations. Now, with apologies to the historically scientific dog named Mr. Peabody and his boy Sherman from *The Rocky and Bullwinkle Show,* it is time to step into the "Way Back Machine." Set it for the mid-1970s . . . and hold on to your bell-bottoms.

If an iMac Was Good Enough for Moses . . .
A BRIEF HISTORY OF CONGREGATIONAL COMPUTING

"It was not so very long ago that people thought that semiconductors were part-time orchestra leaders and microchips were very small snack foods."

—Geraldine Ferraro, 1984 vice presidential candidate

Ms. Ferraro is right. Cultural consciousness of computers is recent. It has been only in the last 20 years that most Americans even saw a computer. The few that we saw up to that time were those that were staples of science-fiction movies—scary devices that ran amok, like Hal in *2001: A Space Odyssey.* Not long ago computers filled entire rooms and overheated so much that they actually caught on fire. Nobody ever thought that computer technology would be where it is today.

Now there is no escaping it. The car we drive to the supermarket is full of computer chips. These chips control practically every function needed to drive the vehicle. When we stop at the service station on our way to the market, we give and get information from the gasoline pump's computer. At the supermarket, groceries are labeled with UPC codes. They identify the products for the computerized scanner. The scanner looks at the market's computerized databases and retrieves the current price. Another piece of software tracks the cost of all the products purchased, adds the appropriate tax, and totals the bill. Still another computer scans the debit card information, tells the cashier's computer that the transaction is complete, and prints a receipt. And, oh, yes, remembers to steal the money from our checking account!

We are used to the technology described above. So why do we need to speak about technology specifically related to congregations? After all, isn't the life of the spirit somewhat removed from microchips? The answer is no. We can see that by taking a brief look at the history of congregations and computers.

9

"GEE, MR. PEABODY, WHERE ARE WE NOW?"

"Well, Sherman," as Mr. Peabody used to say to his pet boy, "we are in the mid-1970s." That is when a few congregations, generally very large mainline churches, began buying their first personal computers. Church accountants or accounting managers generally operated these computers. They used them to automate and increase the efficiency of their financial operations.

It was not until the late 1970s and early 1980s that personal computers began finding their way into homes—and clergy offices. Then, as now, word processing was the most popular personal computing application. Clergy started using word processing to type and print sermons. They soon saw the benefit of using computer technology in other writing—Sunday school lessons, articles for denominational magazines, curriculum, and more. Thanks to this increased personal productivity, many clergy then became advocates for the expansion of technology use in their congregations. And so word processing gained wider acceptance and use in churches, parishes, and synagogues.

Computer networks, now a standard for both business and many congregations, were not practical for small offices until the late 1980s. Those early networks usually had one very large (literally) computer connected to several display screens. And those were never color screens—just green or amber lettering appearing against a black background.

Congregation management software (CMS) followed a similar development course. The earliest versions of CMS were not available until the 1970s. These were written only for installation on individual computers. Some of us remember the days of passing computer information from one machine to another on huge floppy disks.

During the 1980s several mainline denominations created and sold software specific to their denomination. That did not leave many computing choices if you belonged to one of those denominations. Then companies small and large began writing specialized versions of software for churches, parishes, and synagogues. Each one used a different database design. Compatibility between CMS programs—and often other software—simply did not exist.

Congregation software for networks appeared in the 1980s. This CMS was first produced for a single large computer connected to several dumb terminals. Back then a dumb terminal was just that—dumb. It couldn't think on its own. It had to be hooked up to a mainframe—techies will remember them as units like the IBM 36, which ran 8-inch floppy disks. They were as big as a coat closet and slow and noisy.

The real revolution of database software for congregations came with widespread use of the Windows operating system. When congregations began using Windows, they began expecting their database software to look like and function like a Windows program. So companies scrambled to create a Windows version of their software. This development cost lots of money. Many smaller companies could not afford the switch to Windows. They were either purchased by larger companies or went out of business. This left some congregations with "orphan" software—software where the parent company died and no one was left to support it. At the same time, new congregation management software companies were born. They created their products based solely on the Windows platform.

Today there are over 50 different CMS products. The latest trend is to create CMS software as Internet-based applications. To use them, a congregation pays a monthly subscription fee and uses an Internet browser to enter and retrieve data. This makes the traditional congregation information available at any location connected to the World Wide Web; that is, provided you have the correct identification and password.

Besides the above history, the prevalence of technology today, our desire to help you use technology wisely, and the huge royalty checks we are expecting to get, there are three other important historical factors why we are writing this book.

FACTOR 1: OF MONEY AND MOTHERBOARDS

As good stewards of God's gifts, we are called to use the best resources we can find to fulfill our portion of God's mission. Today's best resources include computer technology.

Just a few years ago we visited a congregation where the office manager spent two days every month typing address labels for the church newsletter. The newsletter had already taken three workdays to type and retype, make a stencil, run off on the mimeograph machine, fold, and staple. It took an entire week each month just to send a newsletter to 150 families! Thanks to computer technology, that same task can now be accomplished in less than a day. This savings comes by using relatively inexpensive software, hardware, and office equipment.

Computer technology represents a vast economic savings to that congregation. First there is the salary savings of a week's worth of work that can be turned to more productive ministry or mission. Second, there is the savings in the real cost of technology, which may surprise many congregations. The initial outlay for technology purchases is something that many congregations balk at. But many of these same congregations, had they been around in 1961, would not have hesitated to buy a new IBM Selectric typewriter for their office. That IBM machine would have cost $450. That is more than $2,800 in 2004 dollars. A complete computer system, including printer and software, costs much less than that. And a computer system is much more productive than a stand-alone typewriter.

FACTOR 2: DON'T GIMME THAT ONLINE RELIGION

We knew a pastor at a large congregation in Indianapolis who always said that he would welcome computers in his office. In fact, he wanted two of them—a matching pair to use as bookends for his study. He told that joke every time someone asked why he didn't have a computer. That joke by a well-educated man masked a fear of learning to use a new type of resource. He is not alone. There has been reluctance to use technology in congregational life, and some of it is out of fear of new technology. Some reluctance is out of the belief that using technology will de-personalize a congregation's ministries. Neither has to happen. Technology used well can become a ministry of your congregation. Our work with computers and congregations has shown that the majority of congregations using and experimenting with computer technology and the Internet are not promoting aberrations of Christian or congregational life. Rather, they use computer technologies to enhance and promote traditional ministries: worship, fellowship, pastoral care, education, mission and community outreach, evangelism, and communications.

We wish that we could report that we were successful in bringing the above-mentioned pastor into the computer age. We were not. Today, however, that congregation's current pastoral staff uses e-mail as the primary tool to communicate pastoral care needs and information to each other—much like the first pastor could have.

FACTOR 3: SPECIALIZED SOFTWARE

In addition to CMS, there is some technology, mainly software, specifically produced for congregations, churches, synagogues, and parachurch organizations. There has been an explosion in other kinds of software produced for congregations. Most notable among those new types is the software that companies have developed to assist in visual presentations for worship and educational software for children, youth, and adults. These products can be found in bookstores, through traditional publishing houses, and on the Internet. Some titles are even available at electronics superstores.

Because it is a relatively specialized market, there are fewer printed resources—books, magazines, and advertisements—that have information about these software options. And there are even fewer resources to help you choose which one may be the best for your congregation.

Those are some of the reasons why we are writing this book. Your congregation is already using technology in one form or another. It is everywhere we go, work, and play. And it is changing fast. You already know that. So, while an iMac may have been good enough for Moses (that is, Moses Smith at Williamsburg Wesleyan Church), it is probably not good enough for you. *40 Days and 40 Bytes* will help you wrestle with the "how-best" question: How is it best to incorporate these tools into the modern-day ministry and faith life of your church, parish, or synagogue? But first we need to give a little vocabulary lesson.

⓪③

Of *Heilsgeschicte* and Hard Drives
LEARNING BASIC COMPUTER LINGO

> Freenet dynamically replicates and relocates information in response to demand to provide efficient service and minimal bandwidth usage regardless of load.
>
> —Freenet Web site

Big, scary words are among the things prospective pastors, rabbis, and others learn in seminary. Like the one in our chapter title: *Heilsgeschicte.* It's a German word literally translated "salvation history" or "sacred history" (*heils* is translated "sacred"; *geschichte,* "history"). Used primarily as a way to see scripture as the story of God's redeeming acts in history, it's more than a big, scary word. It's important. And clergy throw it about to prove to lay folks that they went to seminary.

So what's *heilsgeschicte* got to do with computers and congregations? Well, at one level, we could say that the idea of "salvation history" is important to your congregational computing system's well-being. It means you should "save" your "history"—or back it up. But that will be explored in chapter 12.

What it means for us now is this: Seminarians and clergy all know what *heilsgeschicte* means. They use it to talk to each other in class and conversation, but it leaves most lay folk out in the cold. Likewise, computer people have their own language. Some words—such as mouse—mean something completely different in the computer world than they do in the real world. So we're going use this chapter to get us all using the same words in the same way.

That's because we want to make sure you, as the reader, and we, as teachers, are speaking the same language—or at least make sure you understand what we're saying. Some of this may seem very basic and even a little silly. But understanding this language will be important when communicating with technology professionals later . . . and impressing your nontechie friends now.

HARDWARE

Let's start with *hardware*. Though a jokester named Jeff Pesis once defined it as "the parts of a computer system that can be kicked," it's a bit more than that. Put simply, hardware is physical stuff—the pieces of a computer in your office that you can touch—or kick.

Inside Stuff

First is the *central processing unit* or *CPU*. It is the biggest part—that computer box-like thing that sits on your desk or floor. Though there are more things inside the box besides the CPU (you'll find a list of them in the glossary), when we refer to the CPU in this book, we're talking about the whole package.

Inside the CPU is a small box called the *hard drive*. It stores information. Storage is the operative word here. Think of it as the closet of your computer. It's where you keep things for easy access.

Hard drives are designated by size. Currently, common drive sizes range from 20Gb (Gb stands for gigabytes; see the glossary) to over 200Gb. To put this storage capacity in perspective, this entire book is about 8Mb (megabytes). A 20Gb hard drive could hold over 2,500 copies of this book or approximately 1 million average-size word-processing documents. That's a lot of paper in the closet!

One of the slots in the CPU is usually a *floppy disk drive*. Just like a hard drive, a floppy disk drive is used for storage. The primary difference is that a floppy is portable storage—it can be moved from one machine to another—and it is a great deal smaller. It only holds 1.44Mb. Again, using our 20Gb hard drive comparison, the hard drive could hold 14,222 floppy disks. You would need almost seven floppy disks to hold this book.

It's important to note here the difference between storage and memory. That's because these terms are often misused. Hard drives, floppy disks, and other peripherals such as Zip drives are storage—not memory. Memory, at least in regard to computers, refers to RAM (random access memory). To make a human analogy, let's say you are walking through the airport in Honolulu (wishful thinking) and see someone who looks familiar but you cannot place the face. You strain your brain and finally remember he is an acquaintance from high school. You've just accessed your hard drive—that place where you store memories.

Now let's say you're walking through your local mall and see your pastor at the food court eating with her family. You immediately know who it is. You've just accessed your RAM.

Although both examples above are functions of what we call memory, computers make a distinction between types of memory. They have immediate access memory (RAM) and memory that needs some churning of brain cells (hard drive or storage). You might make the analogy that hard drives function like our personal storage of accumulated memories. Storage holds things in your computer that are used only when accessed or necessary—memory is information that's used often.

Another slot in the CPU is likely a *CD-ROM*. Like hard drives and floppy disks, CD-ROMs are storage devices. The acronym stands for *compact disk—read-only memory*. The compact disk part is evident; it's a portable small disk. The read-only memory, however, is a little confusing. When CD-ROMs were first introduced by the music industry, they were truly "read only." That means that once information was put on the disk, that was it—nothing could be changed or added. Now, with the advent of inexpensive CD technology, some of these devices give us the ability to write our own information on a disk. A *CD-R,* which stands for *compact disk—recordable,* can have information placed on it. But, like the old CDs, you can only do it once. The information can't be removed or overwritten. If you want to remove or overwrite info, you need to use a *CD-RW (compact disk—rewritable).* These disks can be deleted and overwritten several times.

Compact disk technology uses an array of confusing numbers to designate and distinguish drives. For a regular compact disk you'll see a number like 48X or 56X. This means that the drive is able to read information at 48 or 56 times the baseline speed that was established a long time ago.

Along with the 56X, CD-R and CD-RW drives have a second (and sometimes third) number. Like a regular CD, the first number designates the speed at which the drive reads. The second number is the speed at which the drive writes information on the compact disc. The third (but sometimes second—just to make it really confusing) number refers to the rewrite speed or what's called "internal" write speed. Unfortunately, these designations are not consistent. All you need to know is that the read and write speeds are usually listed as such on the box that your computer comes in.

Almost any new CD device is pretty fast. So do you need to pay the extra cost to buy the fastest? Probably not. You won't notice any difference in the read category. That's because the speed at which a CD is read depends on the speed at which it was created.

You will notice some difference in the write speed. That's because a drive with a higher speed takes less time to write your information than one with a lower speed. But speed differences for current drives are not big enough to justify spending a lot more money to gain a little speed.

Another piece that likely resides in your CPU is a *modem*. Even with the proliferation of broadband (high-speed) Internet access, most of the world still uses dial-up connections to access the Internet. The modem is the device a computer uses to make this connection. Put simply, a modem is a telephone for a computer. It dials the modem of another computer. When your computer dials AOL, MSN, or your local Internet service provider, it's the same as you picking up the telephone and calling a friend. The call is placed, someone picks up the line on the other end, and a conversation begins. In the case of your modem, it talks to a computer that has direct access to the Internet. It's sort of like dialing a friend who then puts you on the phone with thousands of other people at the same time.

There are two types of modems—internal and external. An internal modem is connected directly to the computer's motherboard. It's inside the box. An external modem sits outside the computer box. It connects via a cable. Usually when you buy a computer, your modem is already installed and ready to go. Sometimes, though, you need to add a modem. In this case an external modem is the easiest way to go. Where installing an internal modem requires opening the CPU, plugging the modem into the motherboard, and then configuring all the address parameters, an external modem just needs a power source (an AC wall socket) and a cable connection, usually through the universal serial bus (USB) port or serial port of the computer. Although external modems cost a bit more than internal modems, if you're adding one to an older machine, then the time savings is worth a few extra dollars!

Modems used to have a variety of speeds. That's not true anymore. Today's standard is V.90 and now the newer V.92. They allow 56K (kilobytes) of data transfer between your computer and the one you're dialed to. The truth is, though, that most of the time you will not connect at 56K. Connection speed depends on a number of factors—including the condition of the wiring in your facility, the switching system that your phone company uses, and your Internet service provider's equipment on the other end.

You may see modems offering speeds greater than 56K. Don't believe them. Even if your modem can connect faster than 56K, the Federal Communications Commission (FCC) regulates that this type of analog connection can't exceed 53K. If you want a faster connection, you have to use another technology.

One last option for modems is voice capability. Some modems are voice capable or voice compatible. No, that doesn't mean your computer can talk to you! It means that you can use your computer as an answering machine. Also, voice-capable modems allow you to connect a headset to your computer. Then you can use it as a telephone and dial directly if you have the right applications. If you are planning on doing serious telemarketing for your church, then a voice modem can speed things up.

Outside Stuff

Let's start with the biggest piece of outside stuff—the *monitor*—that television-y looking thing. It works a lot like a television, except instead of ESPN or HGTV it is used to look at all the information and programs stored on your . . . yes, CPU!

The only way it can access any of that CPU stuff, however, is by using one of two other devices. No, they're not a remote—though remote or wireless versions are available. The first is the *keyboard*—that thing you type on. It's laid out just like a typewriter keyboard, but has a bunch of extra keys. They include a number pad, "F" (or function) keys, and cursor keys. There may be more keys or buttons. The manual that comes with your computer will tell you what the keys all mean.

The second input device (to use a techie phrase) is the *mouse*. Since this book is about computers and congregations, we could call it a church mouse . . . but we won't. The mouse is the funny-looking thing you roll around on your desk that moves the pointy arrow thing (called a cursor) on your . . . yes, monitor. And no, we do not know whether the plural referring to computer mouse is "mouses" or "mice" . . . and we don't really care.

If you're planning on putting what is in your computer onto paper then you need a *printer.* There are three types of printers. They either smash, burn, or paint; however, their technical names are not "smash printers," "burn printers," or "paint printers." Instead, they're known as dot matrix, laser, or inkjet.

Dot matrix printers are rare today because they are an older technology. These printers use a print head and a ribbon to smash characters onto a piece of paper. The print quality of dot matrix printers is usually not very good. Some are fast, however, and they are the only printer technology that can be used for multipart forms such as purchase orders, IRS tax forms, and so on. That's why you still see them used in auto and other repair facilities and department stores. If you have an old one in your congregation, don't worry. You're not alone.

Laser printers use heat (the laser) to burn toner (a powdered form of ink) onto the paper. Laser printers come in various sizes and options. They are rated both by resolution (how good the text looks) and speed. Resolution is rated in "dpi" or dots per inch. For instance, most current printers are 600 or 1200 dpi. That means they produce an image that has 600 or 1200 dots of toner per one-inch square of paper. The truth is you can't see the dots. Not unless you get very, very close and have really good eyes. The only thing that's important here is to know that the more dots per inch, the sharper and richer the image will be. Printer speed is rated in "ppm" or pages per minute. Most current laser printers, even the smaller, cheaper versions are at least 8 ppm—they produce 8 pages of printed text in one minute. Larger laser printers, even those designed for use in small offices, are generally around 12 to 25 pages per minute.

Inkjet printers squirt a burst of ink onto the paper to create an image. As you might imagine, one major problem with inkjet printers is that they are squirting ink onto a piece of paper. The squirt can go astray. And some paper is so porous that it tends to spread the ink around the squirt point. Companies use various technologies to combat this spread. Some add an electric charge that freezes the ink in place. Others use heat to do the same thing. The primary advantage of inkjet printers is their ability to do color. Unlike dot matrix and most laser printers, inkjet printers can produce both black and colored images on a piece of paper. Also, inkjet printers are very inexpensive. Many cost less than $100. And just like laser printers, inkjets are rated in dpi and ppm.

The downside to inkjet printers is that although they are inexpensive to buy, they cost more in the long run—a lot more. Color ink refills are expensive. That raises the cost per page (the measure of how efficient, moneywise, a printer is). The cost per page of most laser printers is under twenty cents. Inkjets can easily double or triple that. Color printing is nice. If most of your congregation's work is black text, however, then you are better off with a laser printer.

So, now we have the basic components of a working computer: the CPU (and its modem and storage devices—the hard drive, floppy, and CD-ROM), monitor, keyboard, mouse, and printer. These are the basic components of a system. Later (in chapter 10) we'll discuss peripheral components and options in more detail. We'll also discuss there what you need and what you don't.

SOFTWARE

For now, let's turn our attention to software and operating systems. To paraphrase Hebrews 11:1 in computer terms, "Now *software* is the assurance of things hoped for, the conviction of things not seen." You hope to put in data and retrieve it in helpful ways. You hope to connect to the Internet and see your congregation's Web site.

Software makes that happen. You can't see it—other than the box it came in and the shiny disk you put into the drive—because it is resident on your hard drive. What that means is that if your computer was to get junk mail addressed to "Resident," it would go to the software. It resides, or lives, inside your CPU. There are two main types of software that you need to know about.

Operating Systems

First there are *operating systems.* Hardware is neat and cool, but without software a computer won't work. A term that every computer user needs to know is *BIOS*—basic input-output operating system.

The BIOS is hardwired into your computer. It is responsible for letting your computer know itself. You might call it the computer's self-consciousness! When you push the power button on your computer, the first thing that starts working is the BIOS. It tells the computer that it is a computer. It tells it that it has this kind of hardware installed as opposed to that kind and that all the pieces are working together. It then passes off to the operating system that takes over control of the computer.

The reason you should know about the BIOS is because if it stops working, well, then so does your computer. It would be like waking up one morning and thinking you were a horse instead of a human. You wouldn't work very well either!

Once the BIOS has recognized itself, then the operating system takes over. The operating system (OS) is software. It now enables the computer to function and run other pieces of software.

There are several different operating systems. Most of us can count on the following—if we have a Macintosh then we'll use the Mac OS and if we use an IBM-compatible computer then we'll use Microsoft Windows.

There are other operating systems including OS2, Unix, and Linux. Most of us will use the newest flavor of Windows. What you need to know about Linux, since you may be seeing television commercials or magazine ads about it, is that it is a scaled-down version of Unix. It is gaining in popularity for server applications and some desktop use. Linux is very powerful but it is not designed for basic computer users. That is why, unless you are a serious computer geek, you probably won't be using it in the near future.

Program-Specific Software

Okay, now that your computer knows that it is a computer (has a sense of self) and the operating system has established the parameters for functioning, it's time for the second type of software to start working. That's program-specific software. It is stuff that you usually have to buy and install.

What's often confusing about this is that most computers come with a bunch of software preloaded on the machine. Some operating systems, such as Microsoft Windows, even have built-in software (such as Internet Explorer) beyond the components that allow it (the operating system) to function. Much of the time this software is fairly basic. It does not do all the things you want to do. For example, while Notepad or WordPad can perform basic note taking, you cannot use them for any real word processing.

We're only mentioning program-specific software here. That's because the next two chapters look at that topic in detail. But you need to understand that program-specific software is a vital part of a fully functioning computer system. And, unlike the operating system software that you probably won't change, this software deserves a lot of your thought. You want to choose just the right stuff so you can do your stuff right.

So now you know your *heil* from your *geschicte*—computerwise. You can say CPU, BIOS, and all kinds of other computer terms like a pro. Now that you *sprechen die computer-ese,* it's time to look at what software can do for you.

Technology Goes to Church

A SOFTWARE REVIEW

You know your church has gone over the technology edge when the parish not only has an Internet Web site, but the parish council has discussed petitioning the bishop to change the parish name to "All Saints Domain" and people without e-mail addresses are known as "the needy."

—Internet joke

All those things William Willimon prophesied—computerized Bible games, pastoral-care software, church management systems, automated birthday cards, anniversary cards—are only possible because of that software thing we mentioned in the previous chapter.

There are many kinds, types, brands, and configurations of hardware. It is fun to look at plasma monitors and wireless keyboards. But it is software, not hardware, which makes a computer a supportive ministry tool. In this chapter we will cover things a computer can do—when equipped with the appropriate software—to help your congregation. You may not need all of these. Or you might. As you read this chapter, start thinking about what you currently need done—and what you'd like to do.

We will be giving a broad overview of the types of software here—not specific titles. Some functions listed below depend on the specific types of software you buy. Our objective is to help you see what is possible. That way you can choose the types of software that best match your needs. In the next chapter we'll look at specific software titles.

WORDS ON PAPER . . . AND LABELS . . . AND . . .

Most congregations use their computer as a glorified typewriter. (Remember that $2,800 Selectric?) That is why we are looking at *word processing* first. Business computing's early development focused mostly on letting users type letters and documents more easily and efficiently then they could on a typewriter. That development continues today. Specifically, computer word-processing programs allow users to edit as they go along without whipping out the Wite-Out to correct mistakes. Most people (at least those of us who have used a typewriter) think this alone makes a computer worth its weight in microchips.

There is an oft-repeated statistic that most users only take advantage of about 20 percent of the capabilities of their software. We're pretty sure that that figure was determined by watching people use word-processing software. That's because most people use word-processing software to produce letters. Very few users take advantage of the software's ability to print envelopes and labels, format complex documents (such as bulletins and worship inserts), and do basic desktop publishing. The most underutilized feature is the ability to do mail merges.

Mail merge lets you print many personalized copies of letters or other documents without typing personal salutations or addresses. You only need access to a member database. Many of these databases can be set up as another word-processing document. To do mail merge, you take information from the "data" document and put it in the "merge" document. You print all the personalized letters, the personalized envelopes, and the mailing is ready to go.

DOING THE NUMBERS

Anyone who has ever been a part of a congregation knows how important numbers are—hymn numbers, offerings, attendance, kids in the nursery, and miles to camp on the church bus. That is why many congregations use *spreadsheets*. Spreadsheets have nothing to do with making up your cot at summer camp. (That's "short sheeting.") A spreadsheet is a program that manipulates data in rows and columns of cells. It is used primarily for mathematical and financial calculations. Sometimes spreadsheets are seen as the troubled teenagers of software. That's because nobody understands them. They look a bit confusing. And they require mathematical calculations—especially the ones we could have learned if we had been paying attention in high school. But, like the teenager, who with care and understanding turns out to be a fascinating and helpful person, spreadsheets can be our friends.

Put simply, a spreadsheet is a word-processing document that is divided into rows and columns. What's unique about a spreadsheet is that each cell that is comprised of the intersection of a row and column is a unique piece of information. In a word-processing document a sentence is considered a single piece of information. A spreadsheet sees that same sentence as individual pieces of information when each word is typed into a separate cell. Where this is powerful and helpful to congregations is when viewing or manipulating numbers and financial information.

Let's say that you need to make a report to the stewardship committee or treasury board. You can print out a general ledger from your accounting software. The group does not need most of this information. It can be rather confusing, unless they are used to reading financial reports and balance sheets. By restructuring the information into a spreadsheet, you can eliminate the extraneous data without compromising the integrity of the information.

You can also set up a spreadsheet to do calculations. That can be as simple as adding a row of budget numbers or as complicated as determining average worship attendance for specific times of the year. Spreadsheets can also generate charts and graphs to make confusing numbers and data more understandable.

TEACH ME THY WAYS

More and more congregations seek and use *educational software*. There are so many software titles available for religious education that it would be silly to try and list them. New ones come on the market daily. That is why we are going to look at just a few types of these programs.

Many congregations find Bible and scripture software helpful. This is true for both adults and children. Many of these software titles include visuals such as maps and charts that allow pictorial representation of stories and historical events. There are also titles that allow clergy and lay users to do word searches and study of religious texts.

Besides scripture software, there are interactive encyclopedias with virtual tours, animation, music, and more for Christianity, Judaism, and other faiths. Some faith-based games teach, too. Some religious authors offer software that includes their study guides, workbooks, curriculum, and other resources. Then there is discipleship software, new member software, children's educational software—the list goes on and on.

There are major differences between these programs, which means that you need to choose carefully. Just like we all think in different ways, these packages present their information in different ways—including theologically. Some software is better fitted for an independent Christian congregation than it is for a synagogue. Chapter 5 gives some tips for selecting software.

ARE YOU A MIDI-ANITE?

We all know that music matters to congregations. Today's music ministers, choral directors, cantors, and choir members have access to many *music software* titles. This software lets them easily compose and publish music charts with different voice parts. Some music software lets you select the instruments or voices you need and then sets up your score automatically on a page size of your choice. Others let you enter guitar fingering or transpose everything—even chord symbols—if you change keys. Some let you create WAV (a file format developed by Microsoft and used by Windows that stores sounds as waveforms), MIDI (Musical Instrument Digital Interface), MP3 (Motion Pictures Expert Group 1 Layer 3), and other music files.

Many denominations offer their hymnals on CD. This allows congregations to search songs and lyrics by word or topic for copying them into weekly worship inserts or bulletins.

A LIGHT IN THE DARKNESS

Once you've chosen the opening hymn, there are times you might like to project it on a screen—to raise people's noses from a hymnal or to make it easier for people with visual impairments to view. *Presentation software* can help with that. Presentation software has gained wide attention in recent years. Since we'll devote much of chapter 7 to worship software, we'll just touch here on other uses for presentation software.

Besides using it in worship, presentation software can be used for board meetings. It's one way to wow them while bringing bad news! Seriously, though, you can use presentation software to show steps for an ongoing project in an easy-to-read and understandable fashion. It also shows graphics (pictures, charts, animation) that hold the viewer's attention. Presentation software can also be used in teaching a religious studies class, showing the congregation to a group of prospective new members, and personalizing social events with snapshots of congregational members and events.

KEEPING A LIST

Congregations need to track members' addresses, committee assignments, volunteer interests, giving and pledges, and many other vital pieces of information. *Database software* lets them do that. Much like spreadsheets, database software is slightly worrisome to many congregational users. That is because it seems complicated. It is—if you get into the programming side of it. But more and more user-friendly versions are out there, which is a good thing because databases are especially important in congregational work. In addition to the examples above, other uses of simple data sets are for library management, baptisms, burials, weddings, chancel choir anthems, religious school attendance, and so on. Chapter 6 is solely devoted to congregation-specific database software (CMS), so we'll go into more detail there.

PUBLISH GLAD TIDINGS

Congregations create bulletins, newsletters, posters, postcards, calendars, and many other visual documents. That's where *desktop publishing software* can help. The desktop publishing possibilities in congregations are vast. Almost anything that you pay a professional print shop to do (such as graphic design, layout, or basic printing) can be done using desktop publishing software.

People wonder why they should use desktop publishing software for such jobs instead of word-processing software. Put simply, it's a lot easier!

Desktop publishing software allows the user to easily—and we emphasize easily—move blocks of text, pictures, borders, and so forth around in a document. If you have ever tried to edit a word-processing document that contained pictures or columns of text, then you know it is not always easy.

With desktop publishing software, though, you simply "grab" a column of text or picture and "drag" it to where you need it in the document. If the column is too long, then a quick mouse adjustment shortens it to fit in its new area.

Creating weekly bulletins with desktop publishing software not only produces better results, but it is done in a fraction of the time word processing would take. And without the usual compromises made because, "I just gave up trying to put the information where I wanted it."

We will introduce you to desktop publishing software that is congregation friendly in the next chapter.

SPIRITUAL SURFING

Congregations use the *Internet* more and more—and with good reason. That's because it can be used for congregational Web sites, e-mail, prayer chains, congregational news, online education, delivery of worship to homebound members, research and study, and even sermon preparation.

In fact, a 2000 study conducted by the Pew Internet and American Life Project titled, "Wired Churches, Wired Temples: Taking Congregations and Missions into Cyberspace," found that nearly all of the 471 rabbis and ministers interviewed reported that they use the Internet as their primary source for sermon materials and personal spiritual devotions. We'll talk more about the Internet and Pew study in chapter 8.

Using the Internet creatively in your congregation may require a number of different types of software. Some Internet software is used to view Web sites. Other types are used to receive and send e-mail. Still others can be used for creating online classes or interactive discussions. While we tend to think of the Internet as monolithic, it in fact is a wide range of services and opportunities—and challenges.

ANSWERING THE CALL

When Willimon joked that, "Every day our computer pulls people's names and makes a personal call to them (using a recording of my voice) . . ." he was pointing to a new technology—*telephony software*. Telephony is not only a new concept, it is a new word as well. Telephony is combining telephone services with computers and data. In its simplest form, it uses a computer as a telephone or answering machine. In more elaborate installations, telephony allows the delivery of all messaging—e-mail, voicemail, and fax—to a user's desktop. Through one software interface (usually an e-mail client), a user can read e-mail, listen to voicemail, and read faxes. This helps with workflow and time management. Just think of the convenience of having e-mail, voice mail, and faxes all in one place.

The phone tree is one telephony device that has a long history with congregations. A phone tree is sort of a reverse answering machine. It sends one message to many recipients. Let's say that you want to remind your grounds committee of an upcoming meeting. Rather than placing 10 individual phone calls, a prerecorded message is automatically delivered to each of the members' phone numbers—even if their answering machine picks up. These devices are quite handy for winter service cancellations when a few hardy souls need to make a lot of phone calls.

DO YOU HEAR WHAT I HEAR?

The last type of software we'll talk about here is *voice recognition software*. As of this writing, this technology is new and fairly primitive. It requires a lot of setup as it gets to know your voice characteristics. After a fair amount of training of personal speech patterns and inflection, these software packages can convert the spoken word into typed text. Some packages are usable and helpful. One of these software titles could be the perfect gift for that pastor that refuses to use her computer, primarily because she hates to (or can't) type. For that pastor who refuses to even talk to a computer, there are small voice recorders that directly interface with a computer and do this conversion. These can be a real lifesaver for the administrative assistant who transposes all the pastor's handwritten notes.

LAWFUL AND HELPFUL

As you see, there are many things software can do for your congregation. The question, though, as we said in the beginning of this chapter, is not, What can all this software do? (which is overwhelming), but, What do you *need* it to do? And do you have the capacity (time, inclination, funds, and so on) to make it work for you? Begin by pretending that the apostle Paul was writing about software to the Corinthians: "'All things are lawful for me,' but not all things are helpful. 'All things are lawful for me,' but I will not be enslaved by anything." It's easy to become enslaved—or at least enraptured—by what software can do. Ultimately, though, you need to think about what you need—and want—it to do. "Congregational Culture Questions" (appendix B), "What Do You *Want* to Do That a CMS *Can* Do?" (appendix C) and "Things You Can Do" (appendix D) will help you with your software assessments.

Now let's look at general software applications that work well in congregational settings.

What Has Bill Gates Done for Us Lately?

GENERAL BUSINESS SOFTWARE AND CONGREGATIONS

Microsoft to acquire the Catholic Church

VATICAN CITY (AP)—In a joint press conference in St. Peter's Square this morning, Microsoft Corp. and the Vatican announced that the Redmond software giant will acquire the Roman Catholic Church in exchange for an unspecified number of shares of Microsoft common stock. If the deal goes through, it will be the first time a computer software company has acquired a major world religion.

—Satiric Internet News Release

Don't worry, Bill Gates is not the new assistant pope. And, in spite of what the title of this chapter implies, not all the software you will use will come from Microsoft! Maybe most of it, but not all of it.

Now that you have thought about what you want to do, let's look at some specific software programs that you might want to use. You will see that many of them come from the secular world. That's because, while there are excellent programs designed specifically for the world of congregations (see chapters 6 and 7), most of the software used effectively in churches and synagogues are the same software packages used by businesses.

There are reasons why commercial software developers such as Microsoft, Symantec, and others are responsible for much of the software you will want to use. That is because it is good, well developed, relatively bug free, and affordable. Commercial titles offer the technical training and product support you need and are dependable. This software works perfectly for a congregation's general computing needs.

While some of the specific information here may be a bit dated if you read this book five years after it first comes out (such as a reference to a specific version of a software such as Office 2003), the software titles we are talking about here have been around a good while. They are constantly being improved. So you can be reasonably assured that they are good, reliable, and helpful.

JUST ANOTHER DAY AT THE OFFICE

Office suites are the most common software packages congregations use. These suites offer a selection of individual software programs packaged into one collection. By purchasing the software in a collection, buyers save a lot of money. The suites include, at the very least, programs for word processing, spreadsheets, and an e-mail client. Other packages include software for database applications, presentations, picture editing, Web site development, and desktop publishing. It is almost possible to outfit your entire congregation's software collection with one suite purchase. And that's sweet.

There are several companies offering office suite packages. These include Microsoft, Corel, and StarOffice. There is no question, however, that Microsoft has the majority of this market. Microsoft's most current offering (at the time of this writing) is *Office 2003*.

There are four Office suite configurations, each with different offerings. All the Office suites include Microsoft Word and Excel (word processing and spreadsheets respectively) and Outlook. Outlook is a multifunction software that does e-mail, address and contact information, appointments and calendaring, and task management.

In addition to these three programs, Office Standard includes PowerPoint for presentations. The Office Small Business Edition includes PowerPoint and adds Publisher (desktop publishing). The most comprehensive version of Office is Professional Edition. It includes PowerPoint, Publisher, and Microsoft Access (database development).

Microsoft has released a new consumer version called Student and Teacher Edition. This is a consumer edition and is intended for noncommercial use only. That means no offices (including congregations) can legally use this version. Do not buy this version for your congregation.

As we write this book, Microsoft offers a program called Charity Open Licensing. Congregations are eligible for this program. This program lets congregations (as long as they have an IRS 501(c)(3) certification) buy certain Microsoft software at a considerable discount. About 20 approved vendors sell these products. Finding one of them is worth the extra effort—you will save hundreds, perhaps thousands, of dollars.

SHOW-AND-TELL

As we mentioned in chapter 4, desktop publishing software can save an enormous amount of time while improving the look of a congregation's printed products. By far the most common software used for this purpose is Microsoft Publisher. It's the most common for good reasons—it's extremely easy to use, comes with a ton of ready-for-use templates, lots of clip art, and is relatively inexpensive. It also has a nifty wizard feature. The wizard lets users apply design options quickly and easily to create high-quality newsletters, flyers, brochures, Web sites, and more. It also has commercial printing functionality. That means that congregations can e-mail Publisher files to commercial printers, service bureaus, and copy shops for printing.

But if you need more power and flexibility, then you might want to look at more comprehensive software packages such as Adobe PageMaker and QuarkXPress. These applications are designed for use by desktop publishing professionals. They add features necessary for producing professional four-color and printer-ready output. Their strength is in generating text-heavy documents such as newsletters, brochures, and flyers. They offer commercial print features. PageMaker also has features for creating PDF files. PDF stands for "portable document format." It is a format that retains a document's original appearance, including text and pictures. This is useful for electronic publishing, since most Internet software programs can read this format. The downside is that these programs' rich features can make them hard to learn. There aren't any wizards, like Publisher has, to help you. That's why, for most congregations, Microsoft Publisher is more than adequate.

IF THIS IS TUESDAY, IT MUST BE BELGIUM
. . . OR COMMITTEE NIGHT

Calendar software is popular in congregations. It's not hard to see why. Churches and synagogues create lots of calendars. Most word-processing and desktop publishing software packages can create basic calendars. But for a more dressed-up look, some congregations use Calendar Creator Plus. This software, which has been around for many years, is loaded with organizational capabilities, calendar templates, thousands of graphics, photo-editing tools, an array of design tools, and on-screen scheduling. It is inexpensive (especially at Internet software shops) and lets you make professional looking calendars in a short time.

Along with calendars comes the ability to schedule congregational assets. These include rooms for various outside activities, tables and chairs, the church van, audio-visual equipment, and other items including sports equipment. Several vendors offer packages that make this task easier. EMS Lite by Dean Evans and Associates is a user-friendly room scheduling and event-management program. It tracks meetings and events that occur in your congregation. EMS Lite generates clear, concise reports. These reports ensure that everyone from the senior pastor to the janitor (who may be the same person, depending on the congregation) is informed and that support services such as room setup and refreshments are coordinated. If you use this program, then, with a quick glance at the computer, the congregation's administrative staff person can pinpoint each event's site, locate free rooms for a last-minute meeting, or book a room for an upcoming reservation. This application can be shared across a network. It can also be user controlled. A user-controlled setup allows different levels of access to the information. That way, any staff person would be able to see if a room was available—but he or she couldn't book it without going through the designated scheduler.

Another software package, Logos Facility Scheduler, goes a step further. It lets users assign your inventory of hardware such as tables and chairs to specific meeting rooms. This means your congregation always knows if there are enough chairs, tables, overheads, and so forth available for upcoming events.

Several Web-based event management services are now available. These include EventU and MyEventCentral.com. EventU does church communications, calendar, scheduling, and resource management—all on the Internet. It lets you do online registration for church meetings or events, and routes resources (rooms, music, projectors, and so forth) electronically through an approval process. This eliminates double bookings of rooms and resources. You can also use EventU to automatically send e-mail announcements of upcoming events—with a feature that allows e-mail recipients to opt-in or opt-out of receiving these reminders. It even lets you receive online donations, pledges, tithes, or sell congregational merchandise such as books.

NOW PRESENTING . . .

We'll talk much more about presentation software geared for congregations in chapter 7, but general presentation software bears some mention here. Most people use PowerPoint from Microsoft. PowerPoint lets you make slide shows with graphics, animations, and multimedia. You can create animation effects such as moving objects, fading slides in and out, and more. Many resources are available that expand the use of PowerPoint beyond its "out-of-the-box" configuration. For example, at Microsoft's Web site, http://www.officeontheweb.com, you can find ready-made templates, clip art, animation, and other free downloads to enhance PowerPoint presentations.

We are finding that congregations use PowerPoint for everything from board presentations on financial issues to classroom presentations for religious education. With a computer and projector, the possibilities for adding visuals to a presentation or lecture are limited only by your creativity. PowerPoint is still the best presentation software available for general use.

CHOOSE WHAT IS RIGHT (JOB 34:4)

Now you know there are office suites, desktop publishing options, calendaring, and presentation software. Do you know how to choose what you need? Choosing software can try even those of us with the patience of Job. Wading through all the types and brand names can be daunting. So how do you go about it?

First, start with the basics—which office suite should your congregation use? A survey by *Christianity Today* showed that this is the predominate type of software congregations use. *Christianity Today* found this especially true for small churches (defined by *Christianity Today* as those with an annual budget under $100,000). *Christianity Today* found that word-processing software is the only type of software that the majority (63 percent) of these churches use.

Choosing the right office suite is important for many reasons. One is that you want to assemble a suite that does the things you want to do. Another is that it's vital to standardize on one version of one platform if you have more than one computer or are on a network.

For instance, if Microsoft Office is the platform you choose, it is important that every user has the same version. That is because older versions are not able to read documents created by newer ones. Getting everybody using the same version may mean upgrading several computers to bring them up to par with the newest machine. This upgrade is worth it. The amount of time that a computer consultant or in-house administrator spends solving problems on multiple versions of Office can easily be alleviated by standardization. Managing licenses is much easier with the same versions installed on all machines, too.

To determine which package you need, start with the most basic collection. Then ask yourself if you need the additional software included in the more comprehensive ones. For most congregations buying new Microsoft software, the Small Business Edition has everything they need (Word, Excel, Outlook, PowerPoint, and Publisher). If several users will be working on some proprietary (specific to your congregation) databases, then you might buy Office Professional for them because it includes Access.

For other types of software, especially those that are a bit pricey, check about getting a review or demonstration version. These are usually available via download from a company's Web site. Or visit another congregation that uses the software that interests you. Most reputable vendors are happy to provide a list of users in your area.

LICENSED TO COMPUTE

Finally, we need to say something more about licensing. Though we mentioned it above, we want to emphasize how important proper licensing is. The sad truth is that congregations often flagrantly violate software licensing laws. Sometimes this is intentional. Usually, though, it is out of ignorance. Although software manufacturers differ in licensing arrangements for their products, a good rule of thumb is that every computer that has a piece of software installed has to have a license for *that* computer and *that* software. This means that if your congregation has five computers with Microsoft Office installed, then you have to have five Microsoft Office licenses. No, it doesn't mean that the church has to buy five boxes of the same program. Instead, you'll buy multiple licenses—one for each machine that you're installing the software on. Your software retailer can advise you whether or not the software you are buying requires multiple-user or multiple-machine licenses and how to purchase them if you do.

We often find congregations using "donated" software. It is "donated" in the sense that someone has brought in her or his copy of a program and installed it on the church's computer. This is illegal. Like we said above, the congregation has to own the license for it to be legal.

We also see congregations that purchase a copy of a software title from a school bookstore because they can get it at a substantial educational discount. Take advantage of such software discounts for your home use— just don't bring it into the synagogue office. Why? All together now—"It's illegal!"

Besides the ethical implications, there are practical benefits to making sure all software is legal. A worldwide organization called the Business Software Alliance (BSA) roots out and punishes license violators. BSA was formed in 1988. It includes the heavy hitters of software development—Microsoft, Adobe, Symantec, Apple, Macromedia, Network Associates, and others— and they are serious about licensing requirements. "Quite simply," says the BSA Web site, "to make or download unauthorized copies of software is to break the law, no matter how many copies are involved. Whether you are casually making a few copies for friends, loaning disks, distributing and/or downloading pirated software via the Internet, or buying a single software program and then installing it on 100 of your company's personal computers, you are committing a copyright infringement. It doesn't matter if you are doing it to make money or not—if you or your company is caught copying software, you may be held liable under both civil and criminal law."

The punishment for license piracy is a fine of up to $250,000 and five years in prison. Additionally, each software manufacturer whose license was violated can collect civil damages of up to $150,000—that's per program! And don't think you won't get caught. The BSA is out and about. It has what amounts to a blanket warrant to enter and check any business for license compliance. Congregations are not immune. They are held to the same standards as any other small business.

While that may seem like bad news (since congregations like to get stuff free), the good news is that many software manufacturers—including Microsoft, as we noted earlier—have special pricing for nonprofits. So it's not worth breaking the law.

BETTER LIVING ELECTRONICALLY

All in all, Bill Gates and his fellow business software developers have done quite a lot for congregations. Their products perform reliably, they do (mostly) what we need them to do, and they don't break the budget doing it. They continue to invest millions of dollars into developing software that churches, synagogues, and mosques will be able to use well. But there are a wide range of congregational needs and tasks that Gates and the others aren't interested in providing software for. Fortunately, smaller software developers are. We'll look at them in the next two chapters.

0 6

Managing Your Congregation

CONGREGATIONAL MANAGEMENT SOFTWARE

If a shepherd has a hundred sheep, and one of them has gone astray, does he not leave the ninety-nine on the mountains and go in search of the one that went astray?

—Matthew 18:12

Many of us know this story. And the question a church member might ask is, "But how did the shepherd know that he had one hundred sheep and one had gone astray?" If he belonged to one of today's congregations, the answer might be that the shepherd's congregation management software said so.

That's because congregation management software (CMS) lets a congregation keep and use information related to activities of the parish—including its people, money, and physical assets. Gone are the days when you had to be a programmer or hire a programmer to keep track of the flock. Most of today's CMS consists of a database and a series of interactive computer programs. These let any user, even a nontechnical person, put in and take out information. Almost anyone with a basic understanding of computers can find a CMS product that will enhance their ministry's efficiency and effectiveness. And there is now software available for just about any congregation—large and small, rich and not-so-rich, computer savvy and computer beginner.

So what exactly can a CMS do? Let's begin by looking at the three areas listed above—people, money, and physical assets.

PEOPLE

At its core a CMS keeps basic information about individuals and families. Examples of this information include names, addresses, family relationships, birth dates, gender, and membership status. Also included are alternate addresses (work, college, or summer home), telephone numbers, e-mail addresses, and other points of contact with each person.

39

Another type of information describes the ways a person connects with your congregation. This includes the person's participation in small groups, committee service, leadership positions, and other congregational activities. CMS lets you track a person's involvement in vestry, personnel committee, lay leader, adult choir, Wednesday Bible study, or whatever activities and committees your congregation has. This type of information often includes a term of service, with specific start and end dates—data that nominating or personnel committees find especially helpful.

A third type of data identifies the skills, talents, and gifts that a person brings to the congregation's service and volunteer opportunities. This information may be acquired through a spiritual gifts inventory, interviews with new members, or filling out a volunteer opportunity form. Whatever the source, the information is usually organized into several main categories and subcategories and may be accompanied by an indication of skill level or experience.

These three types of information are usually contained in the same area of the database, generally labeled "People" or "Membership."

Recording attendance for worship and other congregational events is another common CMS feature. Maybe your congregation has several different weekly worship services and you want to follow someone's attendance (or absence) at different worship events. CMS can help you do that. You may also keep attendance at church school classes, committee meetings, or leadership training events.

A good CMS provides convenient ways to use all of this "people" information to target specific groups or individuals in the congregation. It helps you identify who has missed worship for the past six weeks or has a birthday this month. It even identifies people who are willing to teach a church school class in the coming year.

This process is usually called a *query* or *search* function. In addition to the query function, CMS offers a variety of output options so you can incorporate the information in your congregational ministry—labels, reports, mail merges, directories, mass e-mails, and others. Your congregation's monthly newsletter can include a list of all those members who have a birthday in the current month. Labels can be generated so that a birthday postcard is mailed to each person on the list.

MONEY

Congregations have a moral responsibility to carefully and completely account for every dollar contributed and spent. CMS financial software can help you, at a very detailed level, keep track of all income and expenses to your congregation. This detail can also be summarized appropriately (depending on the audience) to help congregations use information about their money to make wise decisions.

One thing this software does is provide a framework for organizing the annual budget and looking at comparisons of actual income and expense to that budget. For instance, one expense of the children's ministry in a parish might be church school curriculum. CMS accounting software could record an annual budget of $4,000. It could also show that curriculum purchases are commonly made once per quarter in the months of January, April, July, and October for $1,000 each. Then it could track each purchase from the curriculum publishing house by check number and amount, and show budgeted versus actual monies spent by month and year-to-date for church school curriculum. That way the parish's director of Christian education could see a monthly report of what was budgeted and spent for church school curriculum. She could look at similar detail for all expense accounts, along with a summary of all the children's ministry department expenses. The parish finance committee might then see the entire monthly activity for children's ministry summarized as one line in an overall parish financial report, along with similar summary information about each of the other parish ministries.

Almost all congregations have contributors making monetary donations. They may wish to receive a tax deduction for making those donations. The congregation may also solicit pledges and keep comparison records of contributions and those pledges. Sometimes an individual makes an individual contribution. Sometimes two or more people wish to share a pledge or donation (most commonly married couples and families). CMS records detailed information about pledges and contributions, and summarizes them by person, family, and congregational funds.

Another timesaving function that CMS financial software provides is computerized check writing. When invoices are received, payment information is entered into the computer. A batch of checks is printed each week, signed by the proper person(s), and mailed. To assist in this effort, the software keeps a vendor file with vendor name, address, contact information, and your customer number. This file is ready to automatically print the vendor address and customer number once the name is selected from a list. This saves keystrokes for the person creating checks each week. The software also keeps track of check numbers. It remembers which expense accounts are commonly charged for purchases from particular vendors.

Despite the relatively low cost of commercial payroll services, some congregations want to process their payroll themselves. Financial software assists in this task by calculating gross and net pay, subtracting payroll taxes and other deductions, keeping track of vacation and sick hours, producing information for the bookkeeper about how much tax money should be sent to government agencies, and recording payroll expenses to the proper congregational ministry accounts.

Some CMS offers this financial package or gives you the option of using a commercial accounting software package. We'll talk more about making this decision later.

PHYSICAL ASSETS

Physical assets are those nonmonetary things such as buildings, equipment, furnishings, vehicles, library books, or choral music. Some CMS (and commercial accounting software) packages have a physical assets component. This lets a congregation track purchase costs, maintenance, and depreciation. This feature is generally used for larger equipment and furnishings. As an example, let's say that your congregation has an air-conditioning unit on the roof of the community hall. It cost $11,500 three years ago. Last May the local HVAC shop repaired it for $1,350. At that time they recommended that someone inspect the air filters and clean them out each spring to prevent having another repair bill for $1,350. Some CMS lets you enter this information in a way that reminds you when preventative maintenance needs to be done.

Sometimes there are items that your congregation wants to keep track of, but not financially. You just need to know quantities, locations, dates of use, and so on. Choral music is a good example. Your congregation may have an extensive collection of sheet music. It is often difficult to remember what is in all of those file drawers in the music room—or what the choir sang last at last November's Thanksgiving service. CMS helps you track how many copies of each music title are on hand, where they are located, the composer's name, appropriate season for use, and the last time the music was sung in worship.

Scheduling is another common congregational concern. This usually centers around various rooms in the physical facility, but sometimes includes things such as vehicles and audiovisual equipment. Some CMS provides a resource-scheduling feature. This is created specifically around the needs of congregations, as opposed to other software packages designed for concert halls or schools or other organizations. The scheduling software lets you schedule the things that are important to you. It can do this for as far ahead in the future as needed. This helps you avoid scheduling the same resource twice during the same time—known as double booking. These modules also make it easy to schedule events that occur multiple times (such as the stewardship committee that meets the first Wednesday of every month), give room set-up information to custodial staff (classroom style, chairs in a circle, overhead projector needed, and so forth), and create calendars for the weekly bulletin.

Non-CMS scheduling software, such as EMS Lite or EventU, was covered in chapter 5.

SO, WHAT'S SO SPECIAL?

In addition to these three areas, some CMS products offer specialty features. These features help congregations manage schools, preschools, and daycare ministries. They model and track in detail a congregation's volunteer ministry or visitation ministry. Roman Catholic parishes can keep a sacramental registry. Hebrew calendars with date conversions are available for synagogues. Congregations with income from operations other than contributions, such as a bookstore, can manage customer accounts, income, and inventory. A congregation can create and manage a reservations system for large events, record who reserved a place, and who made the necessary payment. These are just a few of the specialty applications available in today's world of congregation management software.

There are over 50 different CMS products available today. All offer various combinations of the features listed above. While they may all look similar, and make similar claims, there are vast differences between them, however. Some CMS offers only a people database. Others have complete sets of modules for membership, accounting, scheduling, and inventory management. None are perfect, though. Your goal is to find a CMS product that is a good fit for your congregation.

CHOOSE WISELY, THAT YOUR DATA MAY LIVE

You need to start by matching the capabilities of the software with your congregation's practices. Congregational practices and culture vary greatly. Each congregation is unique. A Quaker meeting is vastly different than a Catholic church—in business practice and terminology. Consider your congregation's "culture"—how you do things and what practices and features form your congregation's identity. Examining and understanding your culture—how and why you do what you do—will help you pick software that matches your needs, rather than making you fit your needs to what a software does or does not do.

For example, do you want or need to keep track of who received communion? Some CMS do this—others do not. Is your congregation large enough (or family enough) to have more than one person with the same first and last name (Joe Jones or Mary Smith)? Does your church use offering envelopes? Some CMS packages require envelope numbers—so you will be stuck with useless software if you don't use envelopes. Look at and learn your current culture—and decide what needs to stay and what can change. For more congregational culture questions, see appendix B: "Congregational Culture Questions." The questions included there are not exhaustive, but will stimulate your thinking.

Next, think about what you want the CMS to do. Naturally, you'll want to keep track of people. But how—by the relationships they have with your church, such as members, visitors, constituents, children and spouse of members, and so on? How many different telephone numbers do you need to track in this day of fax machines, cell phones, pagers, and so on? Do you want to monitor individuals' spiritual gifts and how they use them? Is the ability to print your own directory important? Do you want to put family pictures in it? Is contribution entry going to be done onsite or from a remote location—such as from a member's home? Do you schedule rooms and track inventory? Would you like to do payroll? Are you going to use the CMS on a network with multiple workstations or on a stand-alone computer?

While these questions seem overwhelming, they are important. Too many congregations have bought too much software without thinking about what they want software to do. We know of one pastor who was browsing in a Christian bookstore one afternoon. He decided impulsively to purchase the only membership management software the store offered. It looked good on the box. He took it back to the church, placed it on the office manager's desk without warning, and said, "Here, let's get our membership organized." It wouldn't and it didn't.

Stories like this are too common—and one reason software ends up sitting on a computer network doing nothing or very little. For more questions, be sure to read appendix C: "What Do You *Want* to Do That a CMS *Can* Do?"

QUICK PICKS

Once you've looked at your congregational culture and have a good idea about what software features are needed, you're ready to look at specific software products. So where do you go now? If you do a Web search a bevy of titles will appear. A better way to start is to check our Web site (http://www.centerforcongregations.org/computerministry.asp) for our updated "CMS Quick Picks." Magazines such as *Church Business* and *Christian Com-*

puting regularly feature articles and advertisements for CMS. Your local chapter of the National Association of Church Business Administrators (NACBA) can tell you what other congregations in your area use. Your denomination might have recommendations about specific products. One of the best ways to find compatible software is simply to talk to congregations like yours (size, location, denomination)—either locally or across the country. What are they using now? Have they recently switched from another product and why? What do they like or dislike about their current choice?

KICKING THE CMS TIRES

Many vendor Web sites now have free (or almost free) demonstration versions of their software. Most are working versions. The demonstration version only allows a certain number of data records or has a time limit. That way you cannot download a demo and use it instead of buying the full package. Downloading a demo version is an excellent way of getting to know the product. It lets you see firsthand how the CMS matches your culture. Other CMS Web sites have online demonstrations of program screens and a list of features. A few of the larger CMS companies have sales representatives in your area. They will be glad to visit your congregation and do a live product demonstration. These companies generally do not offer downloadable demos. But if you are interested in their product, they often agree to provide you with a sample, working database as a trial.

We recommend (we'd demand it, if we could!) that you only make a CMS purchase after either working with a downloaded demo or a live presentation. There is no substitute for seeing the real thing. Some CMS Web sites, brochures, photos, and testimonials that look wonderful hide lousy software.

ALL FOR ONE AND ONE FOR ALL?

One common question is: "Do I need to use the same CMS for everything I want to do?" No, you don't have to—within limits. We recommend that those functions that share common information, such as membership, attendance, contributions, volunteer or visitation management, be housed in the same CMS product. That is because too much shared information is needed to make separate databases practical.

Where it may not be necessary (or even wise—depending on the strength of the software and its capabilities) to branch off into other software is in the special functions. For example, you might want to use the financial module of your CMS—or you may want to stick with the commercial accounting package you've been using. Even if you choose to use a separate financial package, all financial functions should use the same software. This includes any financial information about physical assets. The reason is the same as above—you're keeping too much shared information to make it practical to maintain separate databases.

Specialty functions, such as resource scheduling and library inventories, may be provided by the CMS, or may be separate. Advantages to considering these major groupings separately are that you are likely to get a larger number of features that you want for each area and the initial cost may be lower. On the other hand, an advantage to using the same CMS for all components means having to work with only one vendor and pay one maintenance support fee each year.

STICKER SHOCK

To further complicate the equation, you need to be careful when comparing features and pricing. Unfortunately, there is no universally accepted standard language or pricing structure for CMS products. That's one big reason why it's important to invest the time required to understand what features you want, and how the product will be used—including by how many people and on how many machines. Some software is all in one. Others offer many different modules, with different costs. And not everyone names or groups the same features into the same modules. One CMS may include attendance tracking as part of a membership module. Another may have a separate attendance component. Still another may only keep a count of how many people attended worship, instead of the names of who was there.

There is also a difference in the way providers price products for network use. Some ask that you purchase a separate license for each machine installation. Others will price licenses by the number of users (people) who will be logged on to the system at one time. And some simply have a separate multiuser module. Once purchased, you may install the CMS on as many computers with as many users as needed.

HERE, THERE, OR IN THE AIR?

Something else you will want to consider is whether to use a CMS that is physically located on the computer(s) in your congregation, or to purchase one that is Internet based. Most CMS products are made to reside on the congregation's computers. But there are newer products that are strictly Web based. These only need an Internet browser to operate. Some vendors will offer either option. In this case, the Web-based software is likely to be a somewhat stripped-down version of the computer-resident product.

Web-based software is usually acquired by paying a monthly access fee. This varies depending on the number of users, the number of data records, or even the average number of people in worship.

PROVIDE AT LEAST THREE REFERENCES

Another thing you want to do is check software references. Talk to other congregations using particular CMS packages. The vendor or vendors should be able to provide a list. If they cannot, you want to avoid that software. Talk to other congregations in your area about the CMS's quality, ease of use, technical support, and training. Also ask them what they wish they had asked or known before they bought their software. Avoid any software that congregations tell you is hard to learn, has no real security (you don't want just anybody to be able to see or change data), lists people only in alphabetical order instead of linking them to their families, doesn't distinguish well between different people with the same names, cannot track joint contributions, or offers no or little training or support.

HAVING A CONVERSION EXPERIENCE

If you already have a CMS and are looking for a better product, or if you are converting from a generic database, another consideration is converting—data, that is. Determine how the information you have will find its way into the new software. Do you have data that needs to be moved electronically? Or do you want, or need, to enter all the information by hand? Some products provide data-importing tools and instructions that allow you to convert data by yourself. Others require that the software vendor convert the data (usually for an additional fee). Some make no provisions for converting data electronically—which means it all has to be done manually.

I'M FROM TECH SUPPORT . . . AND I'M HERE TO HELP YOU

Never undervalue training and technical support. Training and support are worth every dollar you spend on them. The most frequent mistake made by new CMS users is a lack of adequate training. Many helpful and useful features go unused or underutilized simply because the people using the CMS have not had enough training.

Include a generous training budget and training plan for each person who uses the software. Be sure to include your congregation's volunteers. Ask the software provider what training is available—and follow their advice. Some providers sponsor regional user groups to help both new and experienced users. Be sure to buy and maintain the support (sometimes called maintenance support) offered by the vendor. These software vendors are small, specialty companies. That means they don't have the testing capabilities of a Microsoft. This often reveals itself in undiscovered software "bugs" (see the glossary in the index). The only way manufacturers make changes and fixes is after learning about the need for them based on user feedback. It is extremely important to receive updates to your software if you want to stay bug free and current.

MINIMUM SYSTEM REQUIREMENTS

No matter what your congregational culture or feature list looks like, some key qualities are common to all good CMS products. Even a very basic "people" CMS should:

- Provide easy-to-use data entry and inquiry screen throughout the database
- Contain a search/query function that allows you to select smaller groups of people or other information with your congregation
- Allow for family members with different last names, and the ability to group all family members together in lists or reports
- Easily distinguish among people with the same first and last name
- Include extra data fields for information specific to your congregation (these are called user-defined fields)
- Provide at least one congregational directory report, such as a phone and address list
- Provide at least one contributions statement format that meets IRS reporting guidelines
- Be able to track joint contributions for husbands, wives, or families
- Track attendance (who was there, not just how many were there) for worship services, and print absentee reports for follow-up

A basic "money" CMS (or commercial accounting package) should:

- Model generally accepted accounting standards and practices
- Allow for detailed tracking of all income and expenses
- Allow the user to create and assign account numbers
- Have account and subaccount capabilities
- Have the ability to track several different congregational funds (operating, building, mission, memorials, and so forth)
- Produce standard accounting reports, such as balance sheet, statement of income and expense, general ledger, journal, or trial balance

Both "people" and "money" should:
- Have easy-to-use documentation, either printed or online
- Offer user training and continued support at a reasonable cost
- Be continually improved by the vendor, based upon user needs and requests
- Contain its own security, allowing access to different information and functions through the use of user IDs and passwords
- Have flexible reports and outputs, so you get the information you want the way you want it
- Have a mail merge capability or export information in a format that your word processor can use
- Be compatible with any Microsoft Windows or Novel Netware product

KEEPING WATCH OVER YOUR FLOCK

Remember, you are not picking CMS simply because you have a computer and it looks interesting. You are looking for something to help your ministry. It is not technology for technology's sake. Computers can help you be more effectively engaged in your people's lives. By following these ideas for matching your congregation with the right CMS product, you can greatly increase the congregation's ability to communicate with, learn about, and provide ministry to your members and community.

Then you might find yourself in the same position as one of the congregations that did it right. That church's staff had used a generic spreadsheet to keep track of its members. Feeling it was time to use a CMS, it then asked for recommendations, went through the process listed above, and purchased a great, inexpensive CMS package. The office manager attended training classes and used technical support extensively. Today, the staff credits the software and their use of it with helping the church's clergy and laity to be truly able to keep up with a growing community. It uses the CMS to target communications to specific groups, follow up on those who miss worship services, and uses skill and interest information to match human resources to congregational needs.

That's how you can become not just the person with a lost sheep, but instead, a shepherd who can keep an ever-expanding flock safely within the fold.

⓪⑦

Preaching and Teaching

WORSHIP AND EDUCATION SOFTWARE

> You know your church has gone over the electronic communications edge
> when five-year-olds actually do say "deliver us some email" during the Our
> Father rather than "deliver us from evil."
>
> —www.unwind.com

There are two things that almost every congregation does—worship and educate. And eat. Okay, so make that three. There are specific software titles for each of these—even the eating. You can buy cookbook software that puts your congregation's favorite recipes at its electronic fingertips. While the eating together part is important for any congregation, we are skipping that topic to focus on worship and education software. That is because these two topics lie at the heart of congregational life.

When we worship, we gather to glorify God and encounter God as we meet in community. When we gather for worship, we seek to encounter the Holy One. Each congregation shapes its worship style based on its own tradition, culture, and style. Likewise, when we meet together for religious education, we seek to grow in our faith and to learn how to live in the world more faithfully. Technology is finding increasing use in both these areas. There is a wide range of software that helps in these vital areas of congregational life. And it can help keep our younger attendees from asking to be delivered "some e-mail."

WORSHIP SOFTWARE

Congregations are increasingly using media in their worship services. The more they do that, the more they find that Microsoft PowerPoint was designed for businesses and not for congregations. Just like the specialized CMS market was born out of congregational needs, so too was worship software designed with the special needs of congregations in mind. There are major differences between the products designed for congregational use and PowerPoint.

The most obvious differences between these products and PowerPoint are their ability to "script" a worship service, store and retrieve information such as hymns and Bible text, use church language, and ease of use. Let's look at each of these separately.

Order of Worship

The scripting ability in worship software packages allows the operator to string together the components of a worship service. Just like worship services vary among religious groups, so too will how different congregations script a service. These components may be different media sources such as audio clips, video clips, and static graphics. For instance, the congregation may walk into the worship space and see a single graphic with the church's logo and a welcome message. When the service begins, the screen transitions to an opening song or hymn. The next piece of media may be a video clip or piece of prerecorded audio. Then it's back to a song or scripture verses to support the sermon. All of these pieces are listed in order on the operator's computer screen. The operator simply clicks to the next piece in the script's order, regardless of whether it's a static slide or audio click. And changing the order (as often happens!) is as easy as moving the mouse to the desired piece and selecting it for next showing. Each of these components is listed on the operator's panel like an invisible director's console. It's sort of like when they show the "truck" from the Monday Night Football games!

Sing a New Song—or an Old One

Most worship software packages come with songs and biblical texts. Some are more complete than others. All include at least one version of the Bible. A number of them offer multiple translations for additional cost. Many have a selection of the most popular spiritual songs and hymns. This means that, rather than requiring the operator to type in the text, or copy and paste it from another program, the desired words are at hand. It is part of the worship software. That makes it easily placed in the order of worship.

¿Habla Iglesia?

These software packages speak *church-ese*—they know congregational lingo. They also provide church-specific tasks. For instance, most all of them include a nursery paging system—something that most businesses do not need. This function lets the operator list a note or nursery message on the screen without interrupting worship.

As Simple as 1-2-3

These packages are designed so that regular church folk—not techies—can use them. Most are straightforward and easy to learn. They do not require great deal of technical background or design or graphics knowledge.

STEPS TO SUCCESS

The question is, though, Why use technology for worship? You need to ask this question. We talked about worship software and what it could do before raising the question simply because so many congregations are doing it. That means that many other congregations assume they should be using it, too. They want to rush out and buy worship software. You need to know what worship software does so that you can ask the "why" question and come up with an informed answer. Regardless of when you ask it, it needs to be asked.

That is because many churches have made the mistake of thinking that buying a projector, computer, screen, and worship software will catapult them into the multimedia worship business and attract giga-hordes of generation X-ers and Y-ers. This is a dangerous assumption. Introducing media into even the most progressive congregation is a major shift. If not done thoughtfully, purposefully, and as a ministry, then serious conflict can result. Nothing, other than the color of the drapes or the new carpet, causes as much conflict as changing things about how a congregation worships.

Our advice is to think carefully about using media in worship. Then, if you think it is a good idea, put together a media team. The team can explore the best ways of using media. It can develop ways that are consistent with your tradition and congregational goals. According to Tim Eason of ChurchMedia.net,

> A strong media team is vital to the success of a media ministry. The key to building an effective team is to first establish a vision for your media ministry. This vision should include the spiritual goals of your ministry and reasons for starting the ministry. . . . Once there is a clear understanding of the vision, the next step it to present that vision to your church. It is very important that church members understand the spiritual motivations for using media in ministry, otherwise many will only perceive media in the church as support equipment for "church as usual." This attitude will severely handicap your team-building efforts and the overall effectiveness of your media ministry. If the church understands that using media will have a spiritual impact, other aspects such as funding and manpower will fall into place.

Tim and his organization are a great resource for using technology in worship. His recent book, *Media Ministry Made Easy,* is an excellent resource for a congregation either starting a media team or looking to revitalize an existing ministry team.

If you put together a media team, and decided to proceed, how do you choose from the many worship software titles? Simple. Try before you buy.

The most prominent worship software titles—WorshipBuilder, Media Shout, SundayPlus—are in the same price range—$400 to $450. They each have working demos available. Download the demo versions and use them.

If you cannot use a demo as part of an actual worship service, try creating a scenario that is as close to real life as possible. Make sure every member of the media team has a chance to play with the software. Although the titles offer similar features, they operate in different ways. You may find some more intuitive than others. Also, find another congregation in your area that uses the software that interests you. Attend one of their worship services. Then spend some time with their media team. Ask about their experience with the software. This will be time well spent. If you do these things you will not end up like one of the many congregations that has purchased what looked like the right software only to find that they couldn't use it!

Finally, don't think that just because you are a small congregation, that worship software cannot help you. Worship software offers some helpful solutions to difficulties faced by small congregations.

For example, many smaller congregations have a hard time finding people to play musical instruments for worship. The good news is that some newer organs—and almost all keyboards—have a MIDI port. If not, the instrument often has the capability to add a floppy disk player that plays MIDI files. Since some of today's worship software packages come with MIDI files included, your small congregation will find itself with a treasure trove of music that is prerecorded and ready to use.

Another unexpected advantage for a smaller congregation using worship software is that it is a way to involve younger people in the worship service. Since many of our teens are more computer literate than the other congregants are, it gets them participating in meaningful ministry.

RELIGIOUS EDUCATION SOFTWARE

Educational software titles abound. In fact, there are so many titles it can be an overwhelming task to select a few for your library or Sunday school. Fortunately, many of the educational titles are relatively inexpensive. Many of them cost under 40 dollars.

We recommend that a congregation establish an annual educational software budget. It does not need to be big. A line item of $250–$500 is fine. That gives you enough money to pick up titles as they appear.

Many of these titles are available at local religious bookstores, through denominational publishing houses, or online. You will be amazed at what is available. There is software that lets you experience Jewish holidays as they've been practiced through time and around the world; scan John Calvin's *Commentaries, Institutes,* and other writings; view animated interactive storybooks that combine entertainment and teaching about Bible stories; play Jewish and Christian Bible games for the whole family; learn to keep Kosher; and read an English translation of the Qur'an.

New religious education software titles come on the market every day. As we were writing this book, we received one denomination's newest interactive history and theology CD. You can find reviews of religious education software titles in some periodicals and online. Look for software reviews. At the very least, talk to someone who has used the software before you buy. Reviews of these titles often appear in magazines such as *Christian Computing, Christianity Today, Christian Century,* and *Moment Magazine.* The Internet is also a good source for information. The magazines above each have a site. Also look at Davka (www.davka.com), The Bible Source (www.thebiblesource.com), and Cokesbury (www.cokesbury.com).

Bible software packages are included in our category of religious education, even though these are not strictly educational titles. They are useful learning tools, though, which is why we are addressing them here. While there are not quite as many of these Bible titles as there are religious software titles, choosing one is quite a task. One reason is that, unlike the religious educational titles, Bible software can be expensive. Some titles cost $300 and more. Cost alone is one reason you want to take your time choosing the right one for your congregation.

Another thing that makes choosing difficult is that there is no one best Bible software package. Each has its own strengths and weaknesses. The task then is picking the software package or packages that best suits your congregation's needs and budget.

For instance, some packages include extensive exegetical capabilities. They contain a wide variety of commentary and explanatory textual analysis. If your congregation needs software for children to look up Bible verses, then you probably do not need this analytical capability. You do not want to spend money for these features.

However, if you are buying software for the rabbi or pastor to prepare sermons and lectures, it is a different matter. You want the features above— and maybe some more. Look for titles that not only include analytical texts but also Hebrew and Greek, multiple Bible translation versions, and lexical-grammatical reference works.

In the same way that we each think in different ways, these packages present their information in different ways. So how do you choose? Try them before you buy them—just like we recommend with all other titles.

Many have demos available for download. If you're considering one of the more robust titles, you might want to check with the biblical studies department or library at a local seminary or college. Since their students will be using this software, they will likely have a copy for you to test drive.

Also, make sure you consider training. The more basic software packages do not require a great deal of instruction. They are fairly intuitive and simple to use. The more complex packages, however, are not so accessible. While they are powerful, they are not always the easiest to use. Again, check with local seminaries and colleges. They can be good resources for training. In fact, many seminaries offer Bible software classes open to the public. The availability of this training could be one compelling reason for choosing one title over another.

Another option in this category to look at is Bible software for your Palm or Pocket PC–based PDA (personal digital assistant). There are several software titles for PDAs. Good ones let you do text and topic searches of the Bible in the palm of your hand. That means that soon you will be searching the Apocrypha, Pseudepigrapha, Gnostic Gospels, Greek New Testament, Hebrew Bible, and Dead Sea Scrolls like a world-class scholar without leaving your pew. Of course, your neighbor will probably think that you are playing solitaire or checking your e-mail—no one expects cyberspace scripture.

One final recommendation is that you do not want to limit your exploration of software to religious bookstores and church supply houses. Many congregation-appropriate titles can be found at large computer and electronics stores. For instance, at one Internet software site we stumbled across a program called "Ellis Island." It is an interactive program perfect for teaching a religious education class about American immigration and religious persecution.

A FAREWELL TO FLANNELGRAPHS

For many congregations, the days of flannelgraphs, pull-down maps, and slide presentations are over. More and more of them are using computer technology to handle worship and educational tasks. There are distinct advantages. Song lyrics, if purchased with the software, are correct—no more

"Gladly, the Cross-Eyed Bear" type slip-ups or upside-down and backwards overheads! The maps of the Middle East would be updated with the latest archaeological finds. Congregations are finding new ways to use the increasing capabilities of software—such as concurrent multilanguage support for bilingual congregations with one screen in English and the other in Spanish.

The creative possibilities with worship and education software programs are almost endless. The important thing is to think wisely about what you want and need to do.

⓪⑧

Tending the Nets

NETWORKS AND THE INTERNET

The capitals were upon the two pillars and also above the rounded projection which was beside the network.

—1 Kings 7:20 RSV

Wow, who would have thought that King Solomon included a computer network when he built his house? Okay, so we admit that the verse above probably does not refer to a computer network. The good news is that you do not have to be as wise as Solomon to build one. Networks aren't that complicated. And their advantages far outweigh any perceived problems and issues.

What is a network? A network is nothing more (or less) than two or more computers sharing information. Copying a file to a floppy and then moving it over to another machine is a crude form of networking. It is called a *sneakernet*—for the athletic shoes you wear out running back and forth between computers. Let's take a look at the components of a bit more sophisticated network.

A network is helpful in even the most basic congregational setup. That is because of its economy and efficiency. For example, a network lets you share one large, workgroup laser printer instead of each staff person having her own inexpensive (and constantly breaking) printer. And one staff member can use the color printer while another is using the workgroup's laser.

A network also means that users can share files. You can set up a common area of shared files. Then all users can go there to browse, edit, or contribute to documents. This is helpful for adding news notes to a bulletin or newsletter—or inserting a good joke in the pastor's upcoming sermon. If your congregation uses a database to manage membership lists and information, then a network is a must. That is because it lets more than one person at a time view or edit information.

Networks also facilitate Internet sharing. Even if your congregation uses a dial-up connection, a network lets one computer with a modem and phone line enable all the other computers to connect through it. That means you do not have to have a modem for each computer. Each machine then does not have to try to connect to the Web through the one dedicated phone line. That ends all the yelling down the hall for someone to get off the line so that you can get on! Without a network you cannot use that phone line when someone else is online.

Networks also improve the integrity and security of your computing system. If one of the users' machines, for example, is designated the file server, then everyone saves their files to that machine. That means that backups only need to be done on that machine. All the other machines would just hold programs—not data. If those machines crashed, there would not be any risk of losing important documents.

Security can be taken to much higher levels with a server (and server operating system) than with stand-alone computers. Access to information can be given (or limited) all the way down the individual file level. This allows you to determine who sees information and who does not.

NETWORK HARDWARE

There are various hardware pieces you will need if you want to have a network. These include servers, hubs, NICs, and more. We will look at each one in detail below.

Are You Being Served?

First, the *server*. A server is a computer. That is a simple statement for a simple truth. While true server-class machines are different than desktops, in essence a server is just a computer. There is a difference between consumer and business-class computers (see the next chapter). Likewise, a server-class computer has some unique characteristics.

A server is designed to run all the time without stopping and without having problems. At least that is what it is designed to do! A server is designed to run most of the time—and certainly longer than a desktop machine—without anybody needing to attend to it. Using vehicles as an analogy, if the consumer computer is an economy sedan and a business desktop is a pickup truck, then a server is a diesel 18-wheeler! We will explain more about this analogy in chapter 9.

Servers function in a variety of ways. The most common are file servers. File servers are central repositories of documents and other files. If all the users put their files on the server, then it's the only machine that you have to back up. That makes the files safer than when spread about on individual computers.

Some servers are application servers. That means they run a program on the server and not on a user's machine. This type of server, called a client-server model, was standard in the old days. Back then one machine did all the computing. Users entered and retrieved information from dummy terminals. They were called dummy terminals because that's what they were—dumb! They did not do any computing. They just sent and received information to and from the server. These systems are still in use at car dealerships and grocery stores. They are hardly ever found in offices these days. In an office you are more likely to find a shared system (called peer-to-peer). That's where the server does some of the computing—like when you run a report from your CMS—but not all of it. Desktop computers are so fast and inexpensive that this peer-to-peer networking replaced the older client-server model.

In the NIC of Time

So now that you've decided to create a network, what do you need? Every computer needs a device that allows it to talk to the other computers on the network. These are called *network interface cards* or NICs. Each has a port where a cable attaches. The good news is that almost all new computers come with built-in NICs. To connect one computer to another you need a piece of cable called—you may find this hard to believe, it actually makes sense—a network cable. The next step is tying the cables together.

That is done through a piece of equipment called a hub. Today it is more commonly called a switch. This box has a bunch of cable connectors on it. That is where all the cables from the computers come together. As far as hardware is concerned, our network is complete!

NETWORK SOFTWARE

Next you need software. Essentially, all the software necessary to create a network is built into your computer's operating system. That is right, it is already there. Whether you have a PC, a Macintosh, or a Linux machine, all the software you need is already loaded. That does not mean your network will miraculously start working. You still need a network person to configure the machines so they talk to each other. That is because not all servers (or computers) are created equal. Server software platforms such as Windows 2000 and 2003 Server, Novell, and some forms of Unix are different from the operating systems used on desktops. Server software is more focused on security and uptime than desktop software is. They are self-healing, too. That means that *when*—and not *if*—something messes up, they heal themselves. Heal themselves, that is, to the point that they do not shut everything down. They also alert somebody that they need attention.

Having a dedicated server with server software is the best way to go. It greatly enhances security and reliability. That is because no one is tapping away on the machine all day long. A dedicated machine can focus on being a server.

The cost of server-based machines has dropped dramatically. If you shop carefully, then you can buy a server for a little bit more than you would spend on a good business-class desktop computer. Even if your congregation cannot afford to dedicate one machine solely as a server, a smaller-scale network is still more advantageous than not having one at all.

THE INTERNET: THE MOTHER OF ALL NETWORKS

The other kind of net we're going to talk about in this chapter is the more famous of the two—the Internet. Everybody knows about the Internet. So why are we talking about the Internet in a chapter on networks?

Because it fits here, that is why. The Internet is nothing more than a large—really, really, really large—network. Using a very complex strategy of connections, the Internet connects millions of computers in a huge network of information. When you type a domain name, such as www.centerforcongregations, in your browser, you are asking for information on a computer somewhere else. The Internet uses *http* (hyper text transfer protocol) to find that information—called a Web site. Most Internet programming is done in *html* (hyper text markup language). This is why typing in a domain name works—it's magic!

The Internet uses the same basic technology to operate as your congregation's local area network (LAN) that we were talking about above. There is a web of network switches and routers, computers with network interface cards, thousands of miles of cabling, and thousands of servers holding the information you seek when you type in a domain name.

The wonder of the Internet is that it works—at least most of the time! People who manage local networks know that even the simplest network needs attention and tweaking now and then. This attention and tweaking is a real problem for the Internet. That is because no one company or individual manages it. No single entity oversees the whole thing. Instead, many companies manage pieces of it. The amazing thing is that, in spite of that fragmented oversight, it stays together and works. If you have a friend who does not believe in miracles, well, just have them study the Internet and how it works. They will be a believer after that!

Since most e-mail travels across the Internet, we will talk about that here, too. Any time you address an e-mail to someone—be it on AOL or whatever.com—that information is transferred over the Internet to an e-mail server. Some congregations manage their own e-mail servers. Most, though, use an Internet service provider (ISP) to do it for them. Your congregation can have its own domain (e.g., firstchurch.org) while paying an outside company to manage the inflow and outflow of e-mail messages. You don't have to do it yourself. In fact, chances are that you do not want the hassle of doing it yourself.

CONGREGATIONAL WEB SITES

One of the most important congregational uses of Internet technology is for Web sites. Just like other computer-related operations, the level of technical expertise needed to create a Web site has decreased dramatically. Nowadays, if you know how to do simple desktop publishing and computer functions, then you can develop and maintain a Web site. Some desktop publishing software even has a "save as Web page" option.

To use the Internet wisely and well, the first thing your congregation needs is a domain or Web address. In tech talk, that is a *URL* (uniform resource locator). That is the name that has *.org* or *.com* at the end. To get one of these you have to sign up with one of the many registration vendors. Recently the management of the .org designation (which is for all noncommercial ventures including congregations) was given to an organization called the Public Interest Registry (www.pir.org).

There are many companies that can provide (sell!) you a .org domain. The PIR acts as the watchdog for the .org designation. You can locate a registrar from PIR's Web site. Registration requires a unique domain name. You may want to use some variation of your congregation's name. For example, First Christian Church's domain name could be FirstChristianChurch, or First_Christian_Church, or firstchrischur, or . . . well, you get the idea. The registrar will tell you if the name you want is already being used. And it might be. So have some alternate names in mind before you contact them.

The registrar will also assign or ask you the location of your Web site files (usually with an Internet service provider). They will also ask for some money. Don't be alarmed. It will not be information superhighway robbery. The fees are reasonable—often around $25 per month. We have seen some as low as $7 per month.

Once your domain is established, it is time to create your Web presence. There are many books and articles about how to create a Web site. For a current list, visit the Congregational Resource Guide (CRG) at www.congregationalresources.org. The CRG is a joint project of the Alban

Institute and the Indianapolis Center for Congregations. It is a continually updated annotated resource guide developed specifically for congregational use. It presents what we think are the best of the best resources. You will want to check there often for updates.

Internet technology changes all the time. For example, one of the newest models for Web development makes Web site creation easy. It is called the ASP (application service provider) model. It gives a congregation all the tools necessary to develop and maintain a Web site without buying any additional hardware or software. That is because ASP providers use your Web browser (such as Internet Explorer or Netscape Navigator). You log into your Web hosting service and all the Web development and maintenance software is available through the ASP's server. Several of these providers are one-stop shops as well. That means they offer all the Web site services your congregation needs—from domain registration to Web site development. Although the monthly fees for ASP providers are a little higher than a regular ISP, we think it is well worth the additional cost to not have to buy and upgrade software and hardware over time.

Another benefit is that the ASP model allows you to make changes from anywhere when you have Internet access and the right login and password. That lets the congregation's administrative staff edit the worship schedule from the church office at the same time that the Webmaster is creating new pages at his home.

YOUR NET GAIN

Networks are a part of today's techie society. That is as true for congregations as for businesses. The savings in time, frustration, data backup, and information sharing are amazing, and it is as much a fact whether you are talking about networking your congregation's 20 stations—or two. So tend your nets wisely—and you will be amazed at your catch.

Disciples of the Disk

CREATING A TECHNOLOGY TEAM

And going on from there [Jesus] saw two other brothers, James . . . and
John his brother, . . . mending their nets, and he called them.
—Matthew 4:22 RSV

Are you called to mend some nets? If so, you may find yourself a disciple of
the disk. In our previous chapters we have looked at what technology can
do in a congregation and what technological infrastructure is needed to
enable that doing. Now we're going to move from the "what" to the "who"—
the technology team.

Through our work with Indianapolis-area congregations, we have come
to believe in technology teams. What is a technology team (TechnoTeam)?
Well, it is *not* a collection of techno-geeks. Rather, it is a group of people
charged with determining what your congregation wants to do with technology; prioritizing and shaping these wants into needs; creating a specific plan
and timeline; following through with the purchase, installation, and training
needed to make the plan a reality; monitoring and evaluating the newly-
acquired technology as it is put into use; and doing it all over again.

WHY A TECHNOTEAM?

Why should you create a TechnoTeam? Because of the above list! It is a lot
to do. We have learned that the TechnoTeam process works. It enlists the
ideas and support of all aspect of a congregation as it plans how to use new
technology tools. A TechnoTeam also builds wide congregational support.
It gets a lot of stakeholders involved. That way your plan is not just one
person's idea. We have seen congregations where one individual worked
with consultants on creating a plan. They then presented it to their
congregation's board, session, elders, only to find out that individual had no
support for implementation.

A side benefit to the TechnoTeam is that, when done right, it draws out congregation members' undiscovered talents. That is a way that the TechnoTeam becomes a model for staff and lay leadership working together to achieve specific congregational goals. This team model can be used for other program areas in your congregation.

HOW MANY POWER RANGERS ARE THERE?

So how many people do you need on a TechnoTeam? The size of the team is not as important as making sure that all major program and administrative areas are represented. Those are the people we call stakeholders—they have a stake in what happens. The TechnoTeam should have members that represent both the staff and the central ministry areas. Examples of staff positions include clergy, office staff, youth ministers, and librarians. Examples of ministry areas are religious education, worship, and missions.

We cannot overemphasize that you need to have both the key people and the key ministry areas represented on the TechnoTeam. How you decide who and what is key depends on your congregation's culture and method of operation. Begin by thinking about who in your congregation moves projects forward—or hinders them. Look at your committee structure—does it represent who does the work of ministry in your congregation? Or are some of the functions combined? You may not need every committee represented—such as the flower committee—but then again you might. You definitely want the people who are going to be using the technology to be represented on the TechnoTeam. In a small congregation, that may mean that all the staff members are on the team—all one of them. For a large congregation, it will probably be one person who can promote the staff's needs. Like we said earlier, these folks do not have to be technologically savvy. Some technical or technology expertise is useful, but the most important thing about the team is that it represents all your ministry areas and includes key staff people.

It is essential to have a TechnoTeam member connected to the congregation's chief governing body or committee. That is because you want someone who has the authority to get the TechnoTeam's ideas and plans in front of the congregation's official decision-making body. This is especially important as you look at paying for your plans.

Another thing that is important is that the TechnoTeam should be made up of permission givers, not permission withholders. What we mean is that folks on the team should be people with vision, who think creatively about possibilities. You do not want people who say things like, "Well, we bought a computer 20 years ago and it didn't do what we wanted. Why should we buy one now?" You may have naysayers in your congregation—just make sure they aren't on the TechnoTeam. Even—and maybe especially—if they volunteer.

TALK AMONGST YOURSELVES

You want a person with good group-leading skills heading the TechnoTeam. It is far less important that the TechnoTeam leader be a technology guru than one who knows how to facilitate group discussions and decision making. A common mistake congregations make is appointing a technology expert as head of the team without any thought about whether that person works well with others.

That is bad because there is one thing that sets our suggested TechnoTeam apart from the other expert-type committees many of us are familiar with. The TechnoTeam is *not* a committee of experts! It is a team of folks who represent the interests and needs of the entire work of the congregation. That makes the leader's job one of facilitating the work of the TechnoTeam—not one of discovering or implementing technology independent of others.

So what does the TechnoTeam need to do? First, they should run out and buy a copy of this book for themselves and all their friends. Okay, that's what we would like them to do because we want this book to appear on the *New York Times* bestseller list. But since that probably will not happen, instead we suggest that the TechnoTeam begin by following the process we have used with many congregations in helping them chart their own technology future. Here are the steps:

1. Identify how your congregation already uses technology.
2. Explore ways in which technology can be used in each major program or administrative area.
3. Create inventories of technology wants from each area, with a rough estimate of costs.
4. Refine and prioritize these wants into short-, medium-, and long-range needs, from 3 to 24 months into the future.
5. Determine what technology will be required to meet the needs, and what kind of infrastructure is needed to make the new technology successful—training, training, training, backup, backup, backup, tech support, tech support, tech support.
6. Create a detailed action plan for acquiring and learning to use the new technology, with specific identifiable steps and a timeline. This step includes actual selection of equipment and software.

7. Prepare a budget for the action plan. The budget should contain concrete costs for meeting short- and medium-range needs, and a cost estimate for long-range needs.
8. Sell the plan to the congregation, including securing adequate funding for the plan.
9. Do the plan.
10. Celebrate, evaluate, and get ready to do it all over again.

That's a pretty overwhelming list. So how do you get started? Read on . . .

WHAT'VE WE GOT?

Begin by taking a technology inventory. This helps you identify how your congregation already uses technology. We have included a sample "Technology Assessment Form" in the appendices (see appendix A). Take it with you when you do your inventory. Feel free to adapt it to your needs. Look at what hardware, software, office equipment, audiovisual equipment, and so forth you already have and use. What do you have and do not use? Be specific—list brand names and dates purchased. Write down the processing speed and how much memory the computer on the pastor's desk has. What version of Microsoft Office does the administrative assistant use? What are the terms of the office copier's lease? Do you know what features and print speed your copier provides? In other words, do your homework about where you are now.

In addition to providing a good starting point, this step may prompt conversations about what the church staff or committees wish they had or are not able to do now.

WISHING AND HOPING AND PLANNING AND DREAMING

This is the fun stuff—the dreams and wishes. Make sure the TechnoTeam doesn't try to do this part all by themselves.

Ask Around
The most important thing to do here is talk to all the right people while taking enough time to explore the needs. Interview folks about ways in which technology can be used in each major program or administrative area. Do not rush. Make sure that each major program and administrative area gets covered. Take lots of time thinking about the activities and processes that are already a part of your congregation's programs, work areas,

or administrative functions. Then begin thinking, as a TechnoTeam, about ways that technology could enhance these activities or make them easier. Only after you have completed that part do you want to think about new activities or programs.

Back to the Future

Next have each person or committee fill out appendix D: "Things You Can Do." This gives you a chance to dream about what you would like to do that is not being done. Compile the information that the completed "Things You Can Do" forms give you. Then decide, based on your congregation's mission, whether these are wants or needs.

In Search Of . . .

Here again, it is time to explore. There are many ways of exploring—talk to other congregations, do research on the Internet, read magazines such as *Church Business* and *Christian Computing,* look at periodicals from your movement or denomination, and buy more copies of this book. Then call Bill Gates and Steve Jobs to see what they are going to come up with next.

Seriously, though, after dreaming what you can do, have the TechnoTeam address one more issue. "Yes, we can [fill in the blank], but why should we? How does that fit with our mission as a congregation?" Only after you've spent a good amount of time thinking about that important question are you ready to move on to the next step.

A METHOD TO THIS TECHNOLOGICAL MADNESS

Now that you've completed the above steps—you have completed the above steps, haven't you?—it is time to systematize what you have found on your exploring. Begin by creating inventories of technology wants from each area. Assign a rough cost estimate to each item. Organize these lists of wants by program area. Look for similarities—of software, hardware, and tasks. Talk about differences. Conversation among team members may help create more new ideas. This is where some technology knowledge can be helpful. If the TechnoTeam does not have this expertise, now is a good time to invite someone from a full-service technology company to visit with your group. Do not ask someone from Best Buy or Circuit City. He may be able to answer your questions—but then again he might be your next-door neighbor's kid who picked up a part-time job after being turned down at Dairy Queen. You want someone who knows what he or she is doing.

When you get your list of needs, you want to spend some time doing better cost estimates for these dreams. Computer and multimedia professionals really help here. Do not forget to check with other congregations. A church or synagogue doing the same or similar thing that you want to do is one of your best information sources.

GET WHAT YOU NEED

"You can't always get what you want" may or may not be true for your congregation. But it is highly likely that you will be able to "get what you need" with or without Mick Jagger. Especially if your TechnoTeam does a good job at this step in the process—refining the wants into realistic needs, with some sense of priorities.

Refining and prioritizing these wants into short-, medium-, and long-range needs—from 3 to 24 months—is sometimes the most difficult and conflict-prone step in the process. This is where the group skills of the team leader shine—or doom the process. If resources are limited—and in most congregations they are—then everyone cannot get what they want. At least right away. This is place for team communication, negotiation, and compromise. Take time to talk about congregational priorities. Encourage TechnoTeam members to look at the big picture—the congregation as a whole—and not just their area. Then, using those priorities and the rough cost estimates, work toward a consensus as to priority of needs. Then develop a simple timeline and put the needs in the appropriate time frame.

DETAILS, DETAILS, DETAILS!

Since this is a book about congregations, we are going to assume that it is God, and not the Devil, in the details. This is the step where details come into play. If you do not pay attention to them, you will find yourself bedeviled.

This is the time to be very specific about what, and how much, technology you need to buy to meet your prioritized needs. Determine what technology is required to meet the needs and what kind of infrastructure is needed to make the new technology successful. One way you can do this yourself is to use the tools at TechSoup (http://www.techsoup.org). It is an excellent online source of information on technology planning. They call themselves "The Technology Place for Nonprofits." Their Web site is a wealth of information on everything from how to create a technology plan to writing grants for technology funding.

It is also important during this step to take a close look at the infrastructure that is required to make technology work successfully. Some of that has to do with things such as determining what kind of electrical wiring and circuits are needed. Other details are about software and hardware. For instance, you have to decide which CMS is best for you, whose computer you will install it on, and what the recommended hardware requirements are for that software. You also have to decide whether you need a network file server or not. How do you ensure that membership files are backed up and protected from computer viruses? How will the data in your old software make its way to the new software? There are also decisions about what kind of training is needed so the staff and volunteers can effectively use the new software. What are you going to do when you can not get something to work correctly? Where will you go for assistance?

SO WHAT'S THIS GOING TO COST?

Preparing a budget for the action plan is pretty straightforward. Take your detailed plan—sorted by short-, medium-, and long-range needs—and attach a cost to each item. Of course, it is easier if you just need one or two things. Even a longer list is not very difficult, though.

Gathering costs for computer hardware, software, and peripherals is pretty easy. You can get printed quotes from local vendors or glean prices at various Internet software and hardware sites. Prices for technical assistance are harder. There are a number of ways to calculate technical expertise costs for installation and support. One way is to ask a company to bid a firm cost per hour along with the estimated number of hours they think will be needed. Or you might decide to purchase a block of hours at a fixed rate. Or you can have a company bid for specific tasks such as the installation of a file server and workstations.

If you sort your budget into short-, medium-, and long-range needs, you will find it is easier to look at the cash flow needed to fund the project. See appendix F, "Creating a Technology Plan," as an example for ideas.

HAVE I GOT A DEAL FOR YOU

This next step—selling the plan to the congregation, including securing adequate funding—is surprisingly important.

We know that congregational polity and culture vary widely. But it is common for every congregation to have a chief governing group or council that approves expenditures not contained in the current year's budget. If your congregation has already set aside sufficient funds for this project, great. We have found that it is more usual for a congregation's first technology plan and its accompanying costs to be considered a special project that needs approval by a governing group.

That is when the focus of the TechnoTeam changes slightly. Instead of evaluating, planning, and dreaming, the TechnoTeam's job is communicating. Each TechnoTeam member needs to share excitement about the project, inform the congregation about the amount of work done by the team, and highlight benefits of the technology plan. The team also needs to come up with a reasonable funding solution or work with the congregational group in charge of funding. There may be some surprises. In one local church, for instance, the tech team leader was surprised by a visit from a curmudgeonly parishioner. He seemed particularly concerned about this technology project he had heard about, and he asked lots of questions. The leader tried to address them with grace—all the while imagining that she was giving him just enough information to lead his charge against the project. The man thanked her politely and left. He returned to the church office two days later with a check—for the entire amount of the project. He said that he wanted the earlier meeting as a way of assuring himself that the team had done its work. After hearing from their leader, he decided that it was time for his congregation to enter the computer age.

Most congregations embarking on a technology project will not have technology built into the annual budgets—or a sole benefactor. There are other ways that you can fund your project, though. Be creative. Pretend you are the youth group! No, we are not saying you have to hold car washes. But we have seen congregations fund technology through special appeals, golf outings, parish festivals, soliciting small groups of donors who have technology interests, endowments or other set-aside funds, grants from denominations or private foundations, or combinations of these various funding methods. Your TechnoTeam was creative when planning for technology—be creative in planning for funding.

DO THE PLAN

You have dreamed, planned, and now have the money. Ready . . . set . . . go for it! The blueprint you carefully prepared is now the map for all project activities and purchases. Implementation is both the most rewarding and most frustrating part of the process. It is a lot of fun to see new technology being installed and used for the first time. Do not be alarmed when not everything works exactly as you planned. Most will. Some will not. When it does not, remember that there is a team of folks who can help; that is, if you have put it in your plan like we said to.

During this phase of the project, the TechnoTeam needs to monitor the purchasing and installation. You may decide that TechnoTeam members can actually do some of the work. Or you may have decided that they cannot. Regardless, the TechnoTeam needs to stay involved, make adjustments as needed, keep the process on track, and communicate with the congregation about what is going on in their midst

CELEBRATE, EVALUATE—AND GET READY TO DO IT OVER AGAIN

Your project is complete. The TechnoTeam is tired but has a real sense of accomplishment. The new technology is humming along in your congregation. Now it is time to celebrate the work you have done together. This is a good time for your congregation to have a technology open house. Or you might take some time in worship to thank the TechnoTeam and dedicate the new resources to ministry, just like many congregations do when dedicating new Sunday school teachers or other ministries. At the very least, you will want to have a team party. Whatever your fashion, it is important to have a time to be thankful, look at where you've come from, and rejoice!

After a few months using all your newfound gadgets and gizmos, it's time to evaluate the project and each of the new resources. Consider the following list of questions in your evaluation:

- How is the equipment and software meeting anticipated needs?
- Would you purchase the same brands again?
- Would you use the same vendors?
- How have these resources been used in ways you didn't anticipate when designing your plan?
- What have you learned about incorporating new technology into your congregational culture?
- Do you need more training in any area?
- Where do you go from here?

That last piece is the "do it all over again" part. We have learned that, if technology is used well, it becomes an integral piece of a congregation's ongoing life. This means that some version of your TechnoTeam needs to become a longer-term committee or group. Things change fast in technology—and people and congregations often make greater use of computers in their ministry than they thought they would when they first began planning.

That is why it is a good idea to revisit the technology process at least once every two years. And you need to make sure that technology expenditures become a part of each year's budget. You do not want to become a St. James—remember them from chapter 2?

HINTS FOR SUCCESSFUL PLANNING

Being a part of a TechnoTeam is fun, challenging—and hard. So here are some tips for making it a little less hard.

Hint 1: Get Professional Help

No, not personal counseling! Professional technology help. This is not to replace the team, but rather to augment its work.

Using professionals is a sore subject for many congregations—especially in congregations that have technology experts who attend there. Our experience has shown that volunteers are not always the best technical resource for congregational technology products. We'll talk more about this in chapter 11.

We have learned, and so have the congregations we have worked with, that professional help used wisely can actually save money. That is because you are working with qualified individuals and companies. They can make recommendations about implementation, suggest vendors for both hardware and software, and help to manage the project. This kind of assistance keeps your congregation from making mistakes—most often of omission (forgetting something!). Using professional help does not mean there is no place for volunteers. On the contrary, volunteer help—in conjunction with technology professionals—can be a very cost-effective way of handling a congregation's technology needs. Volunteers, after all, know the congregation, its ministries, and needs. Professionals can help take that knowledge and translate it into specific technical requirements.

Hint 2: Whose Job Is It?

Another helpful hint is to assign the responsibility for completing each task or job to a specific person. If technology maintenance is everybody's job, then it will soon be nobody's job. It will not get done. Spread your technology responsibilities between professional resources, lay members, and staff.

Hint 3: Budget Big

Include money for more training than you think you will need. In our experience the most common mistake that congregations make is underestimating the amount of instruction needed. It is disheartening to spend a huge amount of time and effort in planning and implementation only to find that no one knows how to use the new technology. Make sure that staff and volunteers have adequate access to initial and ongoing training. Ongoing is especially important. That is because the group of people trained on hardware or software today may not be the same group of people using them two years from now. Staff and volunteers do change in congregations.

Hint 4: Ecumenical Conversation

Our fourth hint has to do with talking with other congregations. You will not find a better resource than the church or synagogue down the street that is doing what you are planning to do. Find out how successful they are at using particular hardware, software, consultants, training sites, and so on. Ask them what they wish they had known or considered in their planning process. And it's helpful to talk with more than one person—often the pastor's perspective is much different than the business administrator's.

Hint 5: Unplanned Obsolescence

Do not spend time worrying about technology advancing past you. It will. Any hardware you buy should be fine and effective for three years. It is likely that your software will need at least one update in that same period. It may need more than one—especially for your CMS. But these updates can be built in to the anticipated software support costs. (Remember—budget!)

Hint 6: Don't Rush to Grow Up

Our final hint to becoming effective disciples of the disk is to grow your technology with your needs. Do not buy things you do not need today or in the next six months. Plan now to buy later. Compatibility is not the issue it once was. Most hardware and software can easily be added to your system later.

Technology is here to stay. Wise use of a TechnoTeam can help you ensure that it stays a useful and valued place in your congregation. You are now an official "Disciple of the Disk."

①⓪

Finding the RAM in the Thicket

DESIGNING YOUR HARDWARE

SUPERCOMPUTER: What your computer sounded like it was before you bought it.

So now that you know what you want to do, chosen the software you need to do it, have decided to network the computers . . . wait . . . what computers? You do not have them yet. That is because it has not been time to choose the hardware you need to run the software. It is now. You need to know some things about hardware if you want to build a system that meets your needs. That is what this chapter is about—how to find some nonsacrificial RAM in the hardware thicket.

THE SAD STORY OF A COMPUTER'S SHORT LIFE

Before you even think about buying hardware, you need to understand that it is a commodity—and a short-lived one at that. Large companies know that. When they buy computers, they don't spend a lot of time worrying about a machine's purchase price. Instead they look at the *TCO*—total cost of ownership. TCO determines how much a computer costs to run over its lifetime. This is usually factored at three years. Congregations can probably get four, maybe five years, out of a computer, but not much more. You may not want to hear that, but that is how it is.

Studies show that 20 to 30 percent of the total cost of owning a computer is attributed to the purchase price. The remaining 70 to 80 percent is taken up by operating costs such as maintenance, administration, and support. And, as Meta Group researchers discovered, the cost of ownership rises as a computer ages. After four years, hardware failures, driver issues and updates, virus and security problems, application conflicts, and multiple generations of support personnel are the primary things contributing to a PC's operating costs. These usually become problems after the warranty has expired.

This short life span is something that most congregations do not realize. They think the machine they buy will last forever. Well, it may, but it will not be useful forever. There is no such thing as eternal life for a personal computer. After the useful life of a machine has ended, the most economical thing to do is to get rid of it. That is not something that many congregations do. Instead, they tend to pass older computers along to junior staff members.

If you think about this, then you see that it is about the worst thing you can do to an older computer—or a junior staff person. An example of why this is a bad idea is obvious if we take the scenario of passing down the church business administrator's three-year-old computer to the preschool administrator. Chances are you are doing this because the business administrator has outgrown the machine. It is underpowered or lacks the ability to run the most current operating system or business software. So why do you want to pass this machine to another person? All that does is move a marginal machine from a skilled user who has been able to massage it enough to keep it usable to an unskilled, or at least lesser skilled, user who will not be able to use it at all.

Hardware is a commodity. Once it fulfills its useful life span, get rid of it! Or use it as a doorstop on the first warm day of spring. Yes, that goes against the grain in many congregations, where old, outcast stuff from furniture to computers is passed around until it ends up in the youth group room—as if they want it! This is one place where a congregation needs to act like a business. If you factor in the TCO, then at the end of three or four years the computer has paid for itself. It is time for a replacement.

The next important factor to keep in mind is that computer hardware is not a moneymaking endeavor for any vendor. Well, at least they don't make very much money! We say this because some vendors do make money. They do this by overcharging for their products. We'll explain this in more detail in our section on value-added resellers in the next the chapter.

BUYING THE RIGHT FUTURE DOORSTOP

So now that you know that whatever you buy is going to end up as an expensive doorstop in four or five years, what do you need?

You need, at the minimum, a basic *business machine,* which is what most congregations need to, and should, buy. This is because congregations need reasonably fast and current processors, an adequate amount of RAM (memory), ample hard-drive space, a network card, keyboard, mouse, and monitor.

Computer technology changes so rapidly that it's difficult to give help-ful hardware minimums. It is enough to say a congregation needs leading-edge—but not "bleeding" edge—technology. That is, you need hardware that is not more than six months to a year old in design and specifications—but you do not need to buy the newest thing slated for release next week. Next week's model will probably have lots of bugs. That is something a six-month-old model will not have. The manufacturer will have fixed them by then. So be current—not ahead of the curve.

There is a difference between computers designed for home use and those designed for business, like we mentioned in the last chapter. A good analogy is comparing a small sedan to a pick-up truck. If both travel over smooth blacktop, then it is hard to tell much difference between them. But as soon as the road turns to dirt and includes rough patches, the differ-ences are obvious. The small sedan will make it through the rough road—once. Asked to traverse this terrain repeatedly, however, the sedan will eventually fail. The pickup truck, however, is designed for rough-roading. It will keep running without breaking down. Home computers are small se-dans—business machines are pickup trucks.

Base Model . . . or Bells and Whistles?

In addition to your basic business machine, you also need what computer folks call *peripherals*. There are lots of peripheral devices available for com-puters. Some are important in a congregation, and some are not. As with software, it depends on what you need and want to do. Some of this informa-tion may seem like a repeat—and it is, but with more detail. It is important to think about these devices here because you are now in a position to under-stand what you want to do—and to pick the things you need to do them.

Modems. As we mentioned in chapter 3, modems are basically telephones for your computer. They are mostly used to connect to the Internet. Unless you plan on using some kind of broadband access (i.e., cable, DSL, T-1), you will need a modem if you want to browse the Internet and send and receive e-mail. There are ways for multiple machines to share one modem. That way each computer does not need one and a dedicated telephone line.

Sound cards and speakers. Most machines, even business machines, come with basic sound cards built in. These peripherals let users hear the sounds that the computer makes and listen to media such as music CDs. Are they necessary for congregational machines? Probably not. Unless, that is, your network includes a way to listen to voicemails via computer (unified messaging), or if your congregation is doing presentations that involve audio. If that is the case, then you need sound cards. For advanced audio production (such as making and using MIDI files), the basic sound card that comes with the computer is probably not adequate. You will need to buy a more advanced sound card—and maybe some additional software.

DVD players. Put simply, DVD players are for movies. If you are not playing movies at work, then you probably will not need a DVD player in your computer. The exception is if you use movie clips from DVDs for education or worship. If you do this, then make sure you understand and adhere to copyright laws. One lawsuit over copyright infringement will easily wipe out your weekly (or decade-ly) offering! Some experts argue that DVD technology will replace CD-ROMs. They think that because DVDs can hold more data. We have not seen anything happening currently that supports that opinion.

External storage. This includes CD-R and -RWs, Zip drives, and Flash-ROM drives. We will look at each individually.

CD-R means compact disk–recordable and CD-RW means compact disk–rewritable. These devices allow a user to write information onto a compact disc. Usually, since the technology to do this destroys the surface of the CD, it can only be done once. However, CD-RWs allow users to rewrite information several times. That is because they use multiple layers of destructible media. CD-R technology is excellent as a way to move large files to different locations. For instance, let's say your media team designs and programs your worship services at various team members' homes. CD-R technology would allow them to copy all the new graphics and presentations onto a CD. They then bring this to the church for Sunday morning worship. CD-R technology is an inexpensive way of moving large amounts of data (up to 650–700Mb) from place to place. It is *not,* however, a good technology for backing up data. First, CDs can only hold up to 700Mb of information. Tape backup drives, which are explained at the end of this section, hold at least 8Gb. Some easily hold up to 320Gb of information (those are *G*s for gigabyte versus *M* for megabyte). In order to back up 8Gb of data on a CD-ROM, a user would need approximately 114 CDs. Other than being inconvenient and messy, 114 CDs cost $60–$70, versus an 8Gb tape that costs about $35.

Even if economic factors are not an issue, there is another reason CDs are not good for backup. That is because most backup software can be configured to run unattended. That means you do not have to sit there and watch it. But if the media (i.e., a CD) is not big enough to hold the entire backup, then someone has to change it when each piece of media is full. That defeats one of the advantages of unattended backups.

Zip drives and other removables such as CD-Rs are excellent, inexpensive vehicles for moving large files from place to place. Zip drives by Iomega can hold up to 250Mb of information on a disk not much larger than a 3.5-inch floppy disk. The advantage of this technology over CD-R is that Zip drives and other removable media use the same read/write technology as hard drives. CD-Rs, on the other hand, use a special technology to write information onto the CD. Many people have experienced the frustration of copying a file to a CD and then carrying it to another computer only to find that the destination machine can't read the CD. This isn't the case with Zip drives. They work on any other machine that has a Zip drive.

Portable hard drives are another popular method of data transfer. These are hard drives in portable cases. They have an external connection to a computer. Again, these are excellent for moving data from location to location. They do have one drawback—they break! That is because portable hard drives are sensitive to environmental factors such as humidity, dust, dirt, and water.

Flash-ROM drives are a fairly new, highly portable way of moving data. Usually housed in a very small (some have loops so you can use them as key chains) compartment, these are electronic storage devices (versus mechanical storage as in CDs, Zip, or hard drives). A predetermined amount of RAM (memory) sits inside the small housing. These devices are usually interfaced with a USB port. You simply plug the device into an available port on the computer. Now you have 16Mb, 64Mb, 128Mb, and in some cases over 1Gb of new storage available.

Tape backup drives. We saved the best, or at least most important, for last! Tape drives do exactly what the name infers—they back up information to tape. There are several formats available, including QIC (quarter-inch cartridge) TRAVAN drives, DAT (digital audio tape) and DLT (digital linear tape), as well as other proprietary formats. These tape drives use special software to compress and store large amounts of data on magnetic tape. They can run unattended, which means someone does not have to sit there and take tapes in and out.

CHURCH COMPUTERS-B-US

So where does a congregation go to buy hardware? You have five choices—neighborhood computer stores, local discount vendors, direct from manufacturers, discount catalogs and Internet vendors, and local VARs (value-added resellers).

Mom and Pop's Corner Computers

Neighborhood computer stores, as the name infers, are the computer version of the local mom-and-pop grocery stores of old. They are simply locally owned computer stores.

These vendors usually sell computers commonly referred to as *white boxes.* White boxes are generic computer boxes with pieced-together components inside. While these are often excellent computers, unless you know the differences in component quality, they are a risky purchase. Besides sometimes questionable component quality, the greatest disadvantage to these is their warranty and support. Even though many local computer vendors offer generous warranties on their systems, a five-year warranty is only worth something if the store is still in business in five years. One thing you want to check is how long they have been in business in your neighborhood. Ask for a customer list. Then follow up with other congregations who use them. While they are not always the best source for new purchases, these stores can be good places for out-of-warranty repairs.

On a Trip to WallyWorld

Local discount vendors include stores as different from each other as Sears, Wal-Mart, Best Buy, Fryes, and CompUSA. Unfortunately, in our opinion, too many congregations make their computer purchases from these stores. We think this is unfortunate because most of these retailers sell consumer—not business—machines.

A consumer machine is made for people who use their home machines for gaming, Internet browsing, music copying, and so on. It is not made for all-day, day-in and day-out, business computing. While often filled with bells and whistles, consumer machines are not the pickup-truck machines that we referred to earlier in this chapter.

There is another problem with these stores—employee turnover and knowledge. The days when the salespeople who worked in department stores were experts about the products they sell are over. We often overhear salespeople in these stores offering erroneous information to customers. We do not want to imply that they lie . . . often they just do not know any better.

The number of information technology (IT) jobs has curbed in the last few years. But there are still many positions available in the IT world. Knowing this, we wonder why someone who really knows what they are talking about is working in a discount store selling computers when they could be making much more money working in the IT field somewhere else. Could it be that they do not know what they are talking about?

Still, if you know what you want to buy and why, and have shopped around and found the best price at one of these stores, buy it there. Make sure, thought, that you figure the TCO—total cost of ownership. If you buy it there, you will want to get it fixed there. Or will you? Check out their service department's expertise.

That is because there can be a danger in depending on these stores for computer repair. Several years ago CBS's *60 Minutes* did an exposé on repairs in these stores. They had a CBS technician purposely install a bad hard-drive cable. This is a $5 repair. They then took the machine to several stores for repair. The quotes for repair ranged from the ridiculous to the insane. They included replacing individual components at one place to another store recommending a complete machine replacement. While these merchants have improved considerably since that exposé, buyers need still to beware when taking computers in for repairs.

Direct from Our Factory!

Many manufacturers let you buy direct from them. In fact, they count on it. They are good places to buy business machines. This includes Dell, Micron, and Gateway among others. There are advantages to buying hardware this way. One of the most important is that you buy only what you want—no more, no less. Buying directly from the manufacturer allows you to configure your computer (or computers) exactly the way you want it.

Another advantage is service. This varies from manufacturer to manufacturer, but most rate very high in this area. Dell, for example, offers exemplary service on their computers. Their turn-around time is often short. They often offer in-office service. Some direct purchase vendors, though, such as Gateway, require users to ship their systems to repair facilities. We recommend avoiding this type of warranty.

Computerstore.com

Discount catalogs and Internet vendors are one and the same. Almost all discount catalogs have an Internet presence. This includes companies like PC Mall and CDW. These outlets often offer brand-name business computer systems at considerable discounts. They can also offer some basic configuration and support help. For most warranty support, these places rely on manufacturer warranties. But they can act as an intermediary in getting this support work done.

Raising the VAR

Local VARs (value-added resellers) include local and national computer resellers, consultants, integrators, and the like. These companies have agreements with computer manufacturers to resell business computer hardware and offer the warranty support. Many times, this relationship includes installation, maintenance, and support. This can be a convenient relationship when warranty work is necessary. The user calls the same company that sold them the hardware.

The downside is that some of these vendors charge for any nonwarranty work that fixes what's broken. This makes sense . . . sort of. That's because "what's broken" often isn't clear. Is it hardware (their responsibility) or software (your responsibility)? Oftentimes, things that appear to be hardware issues turn out to be operating system issues. The vendor charges you to repair these. The same issue posed to one of the direct-from-manufacturer vendors, however, would be clearly defined after detailed diagnostics over the phone.

It is also important to remember that these vendors sell the hardware as a way of getting service and support work. They do not make money on the hardware. At least they should not. It is worth doing some comparison shopping after getting a quote from one of these vendors. You want to be sure you are getting the best price. We have seen—more than once—quotes from local VARs that offer computer hardware for higher cost than the same equipment could be purchased for from discount catalog or Internet vendors. We have also discovered that individuals can purchase brand-name hardware from reputable Internet vendors for less than the VARs can purchase it.

RENT-TO-OWN?

The final question most congregations have about acquiring hardware is whether to lease or buy. We are not financial wizards (well, Nancy is, but she is too smart to put her opinion in writing). We suggest that you consult your accountant for the answer to that question. We will say that computer hardware defies the economic rule of thumb of buying things that appreciate and leasing those that depreciate. Computer hardware depreciates. But if you consider it a commodity like office supplies, then the expense is negligible in the long run. That is why many congregations no longer consider computer hardware to be fixed assets. They take accelerated depreciation instead of long-term depreciation. In that case, it is important to note that leasing costs more than buying. Since hardware becomes obsolete so quickly, the less spent the better. Leasing also offers no tax advantages to congregations.

CAN I GET AN AMEN?

In conclusion (yes, our sermon is ending), as you get ready to buy your system, you need to remember our sermon's three main points:

1. Computers do not live forever, so do not expect yours to.
2. Buy only pieces you need; gluttony, even for glitz, is a sin.
3. Listen to your mama—shop around! Do not take the first quote you get.

If you follow these words of wisdom, you will be led into the path of computer buying bliss. Now, let us pray—for it will soon be time to put it all together.

① ①

Building the Tower—or Two

ASSEMBLING YOUR HARDWARE AND SOFTWARE

All parts should go together without forcing. . . . Therefore, if you can't get them together again, there must be a reason. By all means, do not use a hammer.

—IBM maintenance manual, 1925

So, you followed all our great advice about buying hardware. You have chosen the software you need. The boxes are arriving. Now what? There are three questions to ask: "Who is going to put the hardware together?" "Who is going to install any software not already preloaded on the machines?" and "Who is going to take off all the junk that came preinstalled that you do not want?"

PUTTING IT ALL TOGETHER: INSTALLING THE HARDWARE

First, who's going to install the hardware? Who is going to physically unpack the computer(s) from the boxes and set it up? Someone needs to uncrate them, plug the plugs into the right places, and get them going. That's everything from hooking up the monitor, keyboard, mouse, and any other hardware you bought, to turning it on.

This sounds like a no-brainer. But if you do it without careful planning, it causes a lot of problems. If you are putting the computers on a network, even a simple one, how you answer some of the questions the operating system asks you on the initial start-up makes all the difference between a good install and a bad one. Make sure that the person putting it all together has it all together, and with the technical skills to do it. This person needs to know if the machines are to be networked or not. User names, locations, and so forth all need to be charted before uncrating and hooking up.

WHAT SHOULD WE DO WITH ALL THESE BOXES?
INSTALLING THE SOFTWARE

Second, who is going to install any software that is not already preloaded on the machines? Most computers, particularly business machines, will not have all the software you want or need preinstalled. Some computers can be purchased with Office and other business software already installed. But any other software, especially congregationally related stuff like CMS or worship software, needs to be loaded. This includes anti-virus software, presentation management software, graphics software, audio and video editing software, and any other specialized programs. Just like setting up the hardware and turning the machine on, if these installations are not done correctly the first time, you will spend many extra hours, and probably extra dollars, getting them reinstalled correctly.

Many software packages ask systems-related questions that users do not know how to answer. If answered incorrectly, the installation can become unstable and eventually unusable. Some accounting software packages launch wizards at its initial start-up that ask questions about your organization and its accounting practices. Data tables are established based on your answers. A bad or wrong answer means the tables might be configured incorrectly. Some accounting packages require the user to uninstall and then reinstall the software in order to restructure the tables correctly.

DO WE REALLY NEED THE
"GALATICA BATTLESHIP DEATH RAY" GAME?

Third, who is going to take off all the junk that came preinstalled that you don't want? Well, assuming you didn't take our advice and you purchased one or more consumer machines, you will find an excess of extra software just waiting to confound your computer. The administrative assistant probably does not need copies of Disney Pooh sampler or Pac Man Extreme in order to generate correspondence for the pastor. It is best to remove this extra software as it can cause problems later. Many times these free preloaded games and extraneous software packages are poorly written. They can cause the computer to do things you do not want it to do, such as change screen resolutions, run slowly, and even crash and lock up.

That is because these programs write information in sections of the computer's operating system. Do not just delete them if you decide you do not want them. Uninstall them. If not properly uninstalled, the information these programs have written can cause your operating system to behave erratically.

These are three very different questions. Depending on your congregation, you may come up with three very different answers than does the congregation down the street.

IT'S A DANGEROUS MISSION. DO I HAVE A VOLUNTEER?

You might have some capable and talented members of your congregation who will offer their services to do some of the above steps. They may want to act as your technical advisors, network administrator, or desktop support person. That is nice—but be careful.

We count on the issue of using volunteers coming up whenever we work with congregations around the issue of technology. We do not fault folks for wanting to use the talents and gifts of members. Designing, installing, and maintaining technology systems in a church or synagogue is not often the place to do that.

That sounds harsh. So let us explain. There are some common misconceptions about the roles of technology professionals. Unfortunately, the professionals themselves often fall into the same pitfalls as the staff of a congregation in assessing talents. The most common misunderstandings are discussed below.

Common Misconception 1

Joe is the CIO (chief information officer) of a major corporation. Surely he can drive and manage our church's project!

Nothing could be further from the truth. Most corporate executives who manage large systems are totally unfamiliar with the technology used in small businesses and organizations. It is often difficult for them to scale down their thinking. In their work environment they manage hundreds, or maybe even thousands, of workstations and multiple servers. Their congregation may have five workstations and a server that doubles as the treasurer's workstation. That is a big difference. Although well intentioned, they often insist that congregational systems be more complex than they need to be. That problem is then compounded by the greater level of ongoing support needed to maintain complex systems. Having Joe on the team that evaluates different vendors and consultants is valuable. Just don't give Joe the final say!

Common Misconception 2

My brother knows someone who is a programmer with some big company. He can help us get our systems together!

Wrong again! We all know that physicians specialize. Technology professionals specialize, too. And just as you would not visit an orthopedist for the flu—even though you could—you do not want to visit just any techie. It is common to assume that because someone works with computers and technology, that they can do anything and everything. That is not true.

For example, programmers program. They sift through endless streams of cryptic coding that eventually become software. It is not unusual for a programmer to know little or nothing of systems. System engineers, on the other hand, especially network specialists, know little about programming. They often do not know very much about desktop applications—especially the kind that your congregation will probably be using. So do not expect a network engineer to necessarily know how to make your spreadsheet calculate columns the way you want.

Sure, there are generalists who have a good background in many different areas of technology. But these are the first people to admit they cannot do all the hands-on work themselves.

Common Misconception 3

Once we get our system installed and working, we will not need outside help.

This may be true, but only if you want things to come to a grinding halt six months after you are up and running. Technologies, especially computers, are temperamental. They need lots of ongoing care. Yes, the initial planning and implementation can be the hardest part of the whole computers and congregation process. But you can create a real crisis if your carefully planned systems are not cared for.

HELP WANTED: FINDING THE PERFECT PERSON
TO UNPACK THE BOXES

Remember Joe, our CIO of a major corporation from misconception 1? Well, here is where you can make good use of his skills. What he and executives like him—and here we're speaking of CIOs, IT/IS (Information Technology, Information Services) directors and managers—can provide is access to resources. They know resources, such as vendors and value-added resellers, who might not otherwise have contact with congregations. These professionals also have a lot of experience working with consultants. They know how to speak the language of these providers. Joe can help you find the right person to unpack the boxes.

TAKE ME TO YOUR LEADER: PICKING A PROJECT MANAGER

Okay, so that programmer who your brother knows is not the right person to put your systems together. What do you do? Pick a project manager. Your congregation will benefit from having a technology coordinator. In some cases this person may do the actual work. This is especially true if it is a small project. But often the project manager's responsibility is just to make sure that the work gets done—and done right. This is a good role for a member of your congregation. Especially if that person is someone who can see the big picture and coordinate the different skills needed to bring the project together.

Fortunately, most church systems are relatively simple. That makes it possible to have one person, or one small company, provide all your needs. Caution is warranted, though. Ask prospective vendors if they have experience working with the software titles you plan to use. They may not be familiar with the exact CMS package you have chosen. Any good technology company, though, should have experience working with proprietary, industry-specific software packages.

YOU GET WHAT YOU PAY FOR: ONGOING SUPPORT

You need to plan for ongoing maintenance and support. We recommend paying someone outside the congregation to install your hardware and software. That way you will have trained, qualified professionals doing it right the first time. This means putting it in your budget, which many congregations do not want to do. The fact is, it will save you money. We know that many congregations spend more money hiring professionals to clean up installations than they would have spent having it done professionally the first time. A professional installer will also have intimate knowledge of your installation and setup. This is critical to speedy system recoveries if something goes awry. Also, having a professional handle this work makes them legally liable for problems and issues that may arise in the future.

A bit of preventative maintenance and technical support will save hours of work and many dollars later.

BUT BOB REALLY WANTS TO HELP:
HOW TO USE VOLUNTEERS

We do not want to give the impression that volunteer help is unnecessary or useless. On the contrary, volunteers, when used effectively, can hold your technology together. One good way to use a volunteer is to ask that person to commit a specified amount of time each week to maintaining your systems; that is, if the volunteer is qualified—knows your system, software, and usage, and knows when its time to call for outside help.

MAKING IT WORK: COMBINING VOLUNTEERS
AND PROFESSIONALS

Using a combination of volunteers and professionals can work—once proper balance is achieved. A good example is a large Baptist church we worked with. They had six or seven workstations, a server, and an assortment of printers and peripherals. Nothing ever seemed to work right. The church had a volunteer who was a technology professional. He volunteered four hours of his time per week. It was a noble gesture. Noble, but also futile.

It was not that he did not have the talents to maintain the church's technology. He simply did not have the time. The four hours each week he spent at the church were spent putting out fires. He never had the chance to do any maintenance or upgrades. Things kept getting behind. Soon they were to the point that they seemed helpless.

Our suggestion was that they seek outside help. First they needed help in upgrading existing systems and getting them to the point that they were using current technology. Second, they needed someone available when issues came up—on call during office hours—who could be dispatched to the church to fix things as soon as they broke.

The church took our advice. They interviewed several companies before making a final choice. This began what we consider the perfect marriage between volunteer and paid professional. The volunteer became the technology director for the church. Any time there was a technology issue, he was called first. Then it was his decision whether the issue could wait until he could address it or if the consulting firm needed to be called. He was empowered to make these decisions. And he was accountable for a technology budget created specifically for this purpose.

There are still times when things might not get fixed as soon as someone might wish, but now the volunteer does what is needed and does not put out fires every time he is in the church.

This example shows that having volunteers as a part of your team is wonderful. Just let pros do what they do best.

TRAINING 101

Nothing is more disappointing to us than visiting a congregation that has spent thousands of dollars on hardware and software and then discovers that no one knows how to use it. It is not unusual to find a church administrator who only knows how to use basic word processing and send e-mail, and who relies on someone else for desktop publishing and getting reports from the CMS. We also often find treasurers who know how to get reports from the accounting software, but do not know how to look up pledge and donor information in the management software.

Once computers are in place, ask, "Who is going to use this equipment?" That may seem like an obvious question, but it is not. Does your congregation have volunteers who might use the computers? Do you have a volunteer or part-time staff person who comes in once a week and inputs all the attendance figures or enters donations? Do these people have all the skills and training they need?

Next ask, "How are the users going to use this equipment?" In addition to financial and pledge information, does the treasurer also need access to e-mail and the Internet? Does the pastor's administrative assistant need to know how to access the many different kinds of contact information in the CMS? Does the rabbi need to know a member's giving history before meeting with them to solicit funding?

The idea here is to think broadly. Don't assume every user has all the necessary skills. A good way to find out what people can and cannot do is to have them complete a computer and software skills assessment. A simple questionnaire can show gaping holes in a congregational staff's training.

Knowing where and how to get training can be difficult. This difficulty is often the reason that staff and other users do not follow through with their training needs. Keep it simple. Begin by looking at local community colleges or adult education offerings. Many of them offer basic technology training courses. Many national vendors also provide full-day courses on major software titles for more experienced users. Do not discount online training, either. This method lets users train at their pace. It lets them stop and start when convenient and their work schedules allow. Also look at nationally branded computer stores such as CompUSA. Many of them offer training classes that can be helpful.

Consider onsite training if you have several users who need the same training. It is often cheaper to bring someone to your facility and do group training than sending four or five folks to a training site.

Individualized training—also known as one-on-one coaching—is a relatively new offering. This is especially helpful as the coaching is done with folks using their own computers in real-life situations. These training sessions can be tailored to the exact needs of each user. While they are often more expensive, at least in up-front costs, so much can be covered in these sessions that in the long run they are less expensive than classes.

Proprietary software, like CMS, is often best learned by having a trainer come to your congregation. Most CMS vendors offer this service. If they do not, then you probably do not want to buy their software. After all, you would not buy a new car from a dealer you knew would not fix it when you had problems. Why would you purchase software that the vendor does not support? You wouldn't. So don't.

WHO CAN DO THAT VOODOO?

Building your computer towers does not have to be confounding. If, that is, you take your time before the boxes arrive. Have the TechnoTeam think carefully about who is going to put it all together—software and hardware. Then decide which parts you can do—really do—and which you will save time, money, and effort by having professionals do. That way you will have towers that work—and do not just babble.

① ②

Eternal Security

PROTECTING YOUR CONGREGATION'S SYSTEMS

> Securing an environment of Windows platforms from abuse—external
> or internal—is akin to trying to install sprinklers in a fireworks factory
> where smoking on the job is permitted.
>> —Gene Spafford, from an e-mail to
>> organizers of a workshop on insider misuse

Security is no longer an option. It is a requirement. The days of relegating security for congregational technology systems to the back burner is over. Security issues have moved from a low priority—as in we will do something but we do not want to spend a lot of money on it—to an area of primary focus. Yes, the same Gene Spafford, professor of computer sciences and philosophy at Purdue University and who we quoted above did say that, "People in general are not interested in paying extra for increased safety. At the beginning seat belts cost $200 and nobody bought them." But, as Gene knows, we use them now because they save lives. The same is true with computer security. It saves your data's life!

Security was a fairly minor consideration when we began developing our Computers and Ministry curriculum in 1998. Back then we gave the topic limited time. We had to present so many other topics that we decided that security could be left to casual conversation. We addressed it with our larger congregations—when needed. By 2000 this had changed dramatically—both for congregations and our approach. With the proliferation of broadband Internet access, "smart" viruses, and hacker attacks, it was obvious that security was an area that needed addressing.

These days everybody knows that security is important. Even humorist Dave Barry writes about it. That shows it is serious. But there is no cause for panic; if you take precautions, that is. The likelihood of someone intentionally causing harm to your congregation's systems is unlikely—but not impossible. People do strange things. If they are angry with your congregation, for whatever reason, or just malicious, digital debauchery is a way for them to "rough youse up."

In the summer of 2001 Gartner Group technology consultants and the U.S. Naval War College decided to see how vulnerable computer systems really were. They determined that, "The Internet has its vulnerabilities, including viruses and hackers, but most could be eliminated if companies followed basic good-housekeeping practices, such as keeping server software up to date" (*The Wall Street Journal,* December 16, 2002, B1).

So, what do we mean by security? Security threats include these three primary areas, which we'll look at individually:

1. Virus issues
2. Intentional attacks or threats
3. Unintentional attacks

I AM SORELY AFFLICTED

Viruses are the best-known security threats. They are also the most likely to cause problems for a congregation's technology systems. Computer viruses, much like human viruses, are germs or destructive genes. They enter a computer system and cause harm. Like human viruses, once in the system they can multiply, grow, and infect other systems. You have to "inoculate" a system to remove these viruses. For computers the antibiotics are called *anti-virus software.* This software searches out the virus. It then scrubs the system until it is virus-free. You cannot stop there. That is because if the system is left unprotected—doesn't get its inoculation booster shot—it is likely to be infected again with other viruses.

Years ago the primary method for infecting computers was physically transferring files from one machine to another. Aaron once worked on a document at home, saved it to a floppy disk, and then copied that file onto his work computer. He didn't know that there was a virus on his home machine. He unwittingly copied it to his work machine. That machine was on a network with 10 other machines. They all got "sick."

Back when this way of transferring infections from one machine to another was problematic, the solution was simple. You prohibited users from moving files between machines. It was easy to keep viruses from spreading this way. Systems administrators just took the floppy drives out of the computers. Problem solved!

Then came e-mail. The proliferation of e-mail made infection much easier. Now, not only was it possible to accidentally infect others by sending them an e-mail with a file, but clever coders learned to implant e-mail infections in an e-mail. All without either the sender or recipient knowing they were there. That meant that anyone could infect a whole office by simply opening and reading a virus-laden e-mail. The Internet has made the problem worse, especially with its high bandwidth and many computers today utilizing always-on connections. The culprits have now figured out ways to introduce viruses without a user doing anything except having a connection to the Internet.

Although sneaky and possibly destructive, it is possible and rather simple to protect from viruses.

The first line of defense is the aforementioned anti-virus software. This software is the immunization for a computer system. Such software has two functions: (1) to prevent viruses from entering a system and (2) if a virus does make its way in, to remove it and keep it from doing harm to the computer system.

There are many manufacturers of anti-virus software. The two most prominent names are Norton Anti-virus (by Symantec) and McAfee (by Network Associates). This software is inexpensive—usually less than $50 per machine—and it does an excellent job of preventing and removing destructive viruses.

There is a catch, though. New viruses are created daily—sometime hourly. It is imperative that your virus definitions—those additions to the immunization software—are updated often. Daily is not too frequent. This is done by connecting to the Internet and downloading new virus definitions. Both McAfee and Norton make that an automatic and relatively easy task.

For congregations with local area networks, we highly recommend one of the server-based versions of these software titles (Norton Corporate and McAfee Total Virus Defense Suite). These packages let the administrator install server software. This then pushes the installation out to all the client machines. That way the virus definition updates need only happen on one machine—the server. The server then updates all of the client machines. This is not only easier to manage, but it's often less expensive than purchasing a desktop version for each machine.

The second line of defense for virus protection is what's called a *firewall*. A firewall for a computer system is the same as a firewall in an automobile. Instead of a piece of steel protecting the occupants of the car from an engine compartment fire, it's a piece of software or hardware that protects the computer user from a virus or hacker attack. A firewall lets a computer user control exactly what is allowed to enter the computer or network.

This can be done with hardware or software. Hardware versions, such as those from Cisco, Sonicwall, and WatchGuard, offer relatively simple, plug-and-play solutions for firewall protection. Normally you can install and have these devices operational in a short time. Software, like offerings from Symantec and Black Ice Defender, do a great job of protecting computer systems from prying eyes. However, we find the software solutions slightly more difficult to set up. If you are protecting more than one machine on a network, then they should be installed on the server or machine that is controlling Internet access.

WHERE THIEVES BREAK IN AND STEAL

The next kind of security threats are intentional attacks. Often called hacking, this type of hazard comes from someone intentionally attempting to break into your computer. They might be trying to get information that might be useful (such as banking information, financial records, passwords). Most hackers just like to cause problems and mischief. The proliferation of full-time Internet connections has given hackers an easier go at their craft. Fortunately, for congregations, intentional hacking is highly unlikely. It is hard to pull off and fairly easy to prevent.

Again, the first line of defense is a firewall. Just as with virus prevention, a firewall keeps unauthorized prying eyes out of your business. A firewall is solid protection from all but the most determined hackers.

Another important way of keeping unwanted visitors out of your network is to use "dummy" IP schemes. For those unfamiliar with IP (Internet protocol) and its intricacies, don't worry—your consultant or technical vendor will be conversant with this terminology. Simply put, this method has you assign a fake or unrecognizable IP address to machines on your network. That means that even if someone penetrates your firewall, the unwanted visitor is stopped there. Dummy IPs make that person unable to access any of the information on the machines or server. It also gives you a little bit of satisfaction knowing that someone out there has spent an inordinate amount of time trying to break into a network—only to find out that they can not access any information.

I HAD NO IDEA THAT IT WOULD DO THAT!

The final type of security threat, which is without a doubt the most destructive, is the unintentional one. As the name suggests, this category includes all those accidental goofs we all encounter. Things like someone downloading a file from home, bringing it to the office, and unknowingly infecting the LAN with a virus. Like Aaron did. Or a user receiving an e-mail that looks like it is from a friend when it is a virus veiled as a friendly e-mail. Like Brent. Or a user checking their home Yahoo or Hotmail account while at the congregation, seeing what looks like a funny video file from a friend, and opening it on their work computer—except that the file contains a virus, not a video from a friend.

These are common scenarios. If they are unfamiliar to you, well, you just haven't been using computer technology long enough!

In addition to being the most destructive, these unintentional attacks are the hardest to protect. Most often these assaults are totally benign. Many come from just plain carelessness.

LAYING DOWN THE LAW

The first line of defense for all these security threats is designing and implementing a clearly stated set of "Acceptable Technology Use Policies." Appendix G shows one example of an acceptable use policy. Everyone who uses a computer in your congregation—whether they are paid staff or volunteers—needs to understand what is acceptable and what is not. Be prepared for some initial unhappiness. Users may see this as usurping their authority. It is often hard to convince someone—especially a pastor who has a lot of congregational authority—that he or she cannot download and install software without the administrator's permission. What they need to understand is that it's about protecting everyone's information, including their own.

It is much easier for one person or a small group to keep track of software installations across the enterprise than it is for each person to be responsible for his or her individual machine. When they still refuse to believe it, then you will have to create an enforcement mechanism. This sounds harsh, but it is something we recommend that you do whether you have stubborn users or not! The easiest way to control your computers is by using group policies. This requires a dedicated server that is running either a Windows NT or Windows 2000 server. These server operating systems allow the administrator to decide who can do what.

For instance, it is possible to prevent users from installing or deleting software, adding or deleting printers, changing passwords, or from erasing needed system files by mistake. Although this may sound too much like "big brother," it is standard operating procedure for most network administrators. It has less to do with controlling what users do than it does with keeping things standardized and simple.

FILTERING—IT'S NOT JUST FOR WATER ANYMORE

Many times when people think of security, what they are thinking of is *filtering*. While it is a form of security, it is the opposite of traditional network security. For example, where a firewall keeps people on the outside from getting in, a filter keeps people on the inside from getting to certain things on the outside. Filtering is used almost exclusively for Internet access. It is used to keep users from intentionally or unintentionally browsing objectionable Web sites.

To filter or not to filter can be a more difficult question than it appears. For office staff, some congregations see limiting their Internet access as a violation of trust and free speech. For others, there is no question that, based on their theological perspective, they must use filtering. These are difficult decisions.

When it comes to children accessing the Internet, however, many feel very differently than they do about staff surfing. Many congregations now have computer labs for kids to do homework or learn computer skills. It is not uncommon for children to stumble mistakenly upon objectionable Web sites. There are companies that intentionally misuse Web addresses that they hope people will try—and erroneously lead them into a site they did not want to access, such as a pornography site.

Filtering is available in several ways. Software such as NetNanny does a decent job at keeping most computers protected. However, they rely on you to make sure they stay updated with the latest database of obnoxious Web sites. These sites, much like viruses, change daily. That makes the software ineffective if not constantly updated.

That is why we recommend filtering services. These install a small piece of software on each client machine. When a user types in a Web address, the reply goes to the filtering service provider first. If the site matches a taboo site in their database, which is constantly being updated, it is prevented from showing on the users' computer without a password. Unlike filtered ISPs, these filtering services can be used with any Internet connection, whether it is dial-up, DSL, ISDN, or T-1.

THE PASSWORD IS . . .

The final—and simplest—method of managing security is passwords. A congregation's network is only as secure as its weakest password. They are often very weak. It is far too common for congregations to allow users to establish passwords that are not difficult to guess. The most common passwords are *password, secret,* and *jamesbond* (really!). Make users establish passwords that are hard to guess—no nicknames or birthdates. Make sure users change them periodically, too. Also, make it clear that sharing passwords is not okay. This sounds silly, but it is one of the most common security weaknesses. Finally, do not make passwords so difficult that they cannot be remembered. If users have to write them down, then someone who should not will find them. There goes your security!

BACKUP, BACKUP, BACKUP (REPEAT DAILY)

After you have protected yourself, there is one last thing you can do. Back up your data—that is the ultimate security device. We cannot say enough about backing up your data—but we are only allowed to put so many words in this book, so we will take just a couple of paragraphs.

Many times congregations do not even think of backing up data. Not until there is an emergency that could have been averted if regular backups were a part of normal operations, that is. By then it is too late.

That is why you need to back up data regularly. Daily is not too often. If your congregation is networked, then you can save everyone's user files on one computer and back that information up every night. If you use CMS and accounting software, you want to back up the data every night. You do not have to back up programs. Those are easily restorable from the original CDs (assuming you own a license and have the original CD). Always store your backups somewhere safe. That is not in a box under your desk or in the server room. Take them offsite. That way, if your church would have a fire and all your computers were destroyed, your data would be somewhere else. It would be safe and restorable. As soon as new computers are online, you could do a simple reinstallation of the original software and then restore the data. You will be back in business.

Too many congregations have experienced the horror of losing all their data with no backup and no way to recover other than starting from scratch. You do not want to be one of them.

There is good reason that this subject belongs in the security chapter. That is because sometimes the last resort to fixing data corrupted by a virus or inattention or stolen password is replacing it with data that has been recently backed up.

There is no excuse for not doing this. Backups are easy and inexpensive. And backup software can be set so that it will run unattended. It can literally save your data's life. There are several very good backup software titles including Dantz Retropect and Veritas Backup Exec. There are different software versions depending on whether you're backing up servers or desktops (or both). Microsoft Windows Server versions also come with a scaled-down version of Veritas Backup Exec already installed. This is often adequate for most congregations.

CHECK FOR INCOMING ELECTRICITY

Security is crucial for today's congregations. If you ignore this topic, then you risk turning your computer into a doorstop years ahead of its time. And that is the best-case scenario. The worst-case scenario is that someone will destroy all your data, steal your financial information, and clean out your bank account.

Dave Barry's "Keyboard Korner" ("the computer-advice column that uses simple, 'jargon free' terminology that even an idiot like you can grasp") of December 14, 2003, suggests three things for making your computer secure. The first is to "get rid of teenagers." The second is to "check for incoming electricity." The final one is to "curl into a fetal position and remain under the desk." This is good advice. Well, it is funny advice. Better advice is to install anti-virus and firewall protection. Update your passwords regularly. Back up your data.

If you do those things, you will find your computers "safe and secure from all alarms."

① ③

I've Got a PC in Glory Land
That Outshines the Sun
THE FUTURE OF CONGREGATIONAL COMPUTING

I think there is a world market for maybe five computers.
> —Thomas Watson, chairman of IBM, 1943

Computers in the future may weigh no more than 1.5 tons.
> —*Popular Mechanics*, 1949

There is no reason anyone would want a computer in their home.
> —Ken Olson, president, chairman and founder of DEC

640K [of memory] ought to be enough for anybody.
> —Bill Gates, 1981

If the experts above could not predict the computing future, what makes us think we can? After all, Aaron and Brent thought that CDs would come and go and everybody would be using Digital Audio Tape (DAT) by now. And all three of us laughed at the thought of PDAs when they first appeared in 1992. That was when Apple announced its Newton—a highly sophisticated computerized organizer that recognized handwriting, acted as an electronic organizer, allowed its users to send and receive e-mail while weighing less than a pound, and cost less than $1,000. *Yeah, sure,* we thought. *Next you'll be telling us that someday the World Wide Web will be used by school kids to find quotations for their term papers.*

So here we are, listening to our CDs, sending e-mail from our PDAs, surfing the Internet for quotes that missed the mark about computing's future. Still, we are going to dare to predict the future of congregational computing—and give you some advice while doing it.

Someday computers will . . . never mind. We are not going to do that kind of technological prediction. Instead, here is our prophecy—technology will continue to grow and change and develop. New products we cannot imagine will be introduced. Many will be useful to congregations. Others will not.

How is that helpful? Just in this way—while we do not know what the future holds, we do know how to deal with it. That is by thinking carefully about the following prophetic statements. Please read them aloud in a properly prophetic voice.

PROPHETIC STATEMENT 1:
YOU WILL BUY WHAT YOU NEED AND NEED WHAT YOU BUY

In the future, as now, the important thing is to remember you are not picking technology because it looks interesting. You are looking for something to help your ministry. You do not want technology for technology's sake. The technology you want is something that fits your congregation's life and mission and helps you be more effective in peoples' lives. Start by matching the capabilities of the software with your congregation's practices. Think about your congregation's culture—how you do things, what practices and features create the identity for your congregation. These include worship, teaching, and stewardship—everything that touches your congregation. Looking at and understanding your congregational culture helps you pick technology that meets your needs, rather than making you fit your needs to what technology can do.

PROPHETIC STATEMENT 2:
YOU WILL KEEP LISTS

We also predict that congregations will use technology in administration and finance. Since the early 1980s many congregations have been using CMS to help them with budgeting and accounting, tracking members and constituents, cataloging volunteer interests and gifts, recording attendance, scheduling activities, and much more. Thousands of congregations nationally function more efficiently and effectively because of CMS technology. This trend will grow.

PROPHETIC STATEMENT 3:
YOU WILL THINK OUTSIDE THE BOX

We predict that congregations will find nontraditional uses for such software—if they think creatively, that is. Databases can do much more than provide mailing labels for the church newsletter. CMS or other database management software can assist congregations as they engage in outreach and mission—by thinking outside (the software) box. For example, a Missionary Baptist church in Indianapolis has been giving away thousands of pairs of shoes to children in need for years with the help of a network of retail stores that donate surplus inventory. The church had no effective way of tracking the names, addresses, and circumstances of the children from year to year, though. That meant families had to take the initiative to find the program. The church now uses a database system, installed on laptop computers, to track donors and recipients. It keeps inventory information about the shoes and each child in the program from year to year. The congregation takes the initiative in ministering to the families.

PROPHETIC STATEMENT 4:
YOU WILL DO IT YOURSELF

We also predict that desktop publishing will become easier and easier. In the past, it has allowed churches to improve the quality and appearance of worship bulletins, newsletters, correspondence, flyers, posters, sermons, and other educational or devotional materials. Most programs required a fair amount of sophistication and training to turn out truly quality materials. That is changing. The inclusion of templates and wizards is taking away the more fearsome aspects of these programs.

PROPHETIC STATEMENT 5:
YOU WILL TRAVEL IN CYBERSPACE DAILY

We also predict that e-mail and other Internet-related messaging modes will play an increasingly important part of a congregation's communication strategy. A whopping 91 percent of the respondents in the Pew report "Wired Churches and Wired Temples" said that e-mail has helped clergy and church members to promote fellowship and community-building communication. We see this growing in usage for sharing prayer concerns, coordinating committee meetings, and providing spiritual advice and support.

Again, creative thinking is called for. The pastor of a United Methodist church in Indianapolis asked during a worship service if anyone would be interested in receiving a weekly devotional e-mail. He was flooded with members' e-mail addresses. These members, after they received the e-mailed devotionals, began forwarding them to friends, family, neighbors, and coworkers. This launched an unexpected ministry that is now a significant outreach for the church.

The influence of e-mail on internal communications, particularly among church staff, is also significant. Again, in the Pew report an overwhelming

97 percent of respondents from churches with high access to Internet communications said that e-mail "helped congregational staff and members stay in touch." For a good example of that, we point to a large church we know. The church had seven staff members. All of them had computers and printers on their desks. Each computer, though, had its own modem and phone line. That meant each staff person had to access their own personal America Online account to use e-mail. Communication between and among staff was entirely ad hoc, ineffective, and inefficient. Their computers were incompatible. The staff members began to think that they were incompatible, too. When the church installed new computers connected to a local area network and to an Internet service provider, the staff was astonished at how internal communications improved. And the monthly fee to connect the church as a whole to the Internet was less than the individual AOL accounts had been.

We predict that other Internet technologies will continue to impact congregational communication dramatically. Many congregations already use Web sites to communicate with members about fellowship and upcoming events. More and more congregations will find new ways to use this amazing technology for in-reach and out-reach. One church we worked with sent its youth group on a mission trip to South America. They wanted to keep the congregation informed about the group's activities. Using a digital camera and laptop, the group's leaders sent daily digital pictures from the mission site. Along with the pictures came e-mails summarizing the group's activities, describing their feelings and experiences, introducing village children to the folks back home, and asking for prayers. The pictures and messages were posted on the church's Web site each day. Back home in Indiana, spontaneous gatherings began taking place. The parents of the youth and others started gathering daily at the church to learn the latest news and to pray for the youth and the people of the village they were serving.

Web-based technology is available that sets up for discussion groups, online learning, and password-protected pages linked to committee minutes or other sensitive material. Chat rooms can be utilized for sermon or Sunday school lesson discussion.

PROPHETIC STATEMENT 6:
YOU WILL LEARN ON THE COMPUTER

We also believe that more and more congregations will use learning labs, which is not something we would have predicted in 1998. But to our surprise, a quarter of the congregations that applied to the Indianapolis Center's computer grants program wanted to either establish or improve a learning lab. Many of them wanted to use the lab both as an outreach program for the surrounding community and as a tool for religious education in the congregation. African American churches that serve impoverished urban areas argued compellingly that many kids in their neighborhoods were left out of the "digital revolution" because they didn't have home computers. Labs in these churches, available for after-school and other programs for youth, helped close this digital divide.

Many parishes and synagogues recognize that the digital divide is generational as well as economic. Some churches are establishing labs for senior citizens as well as for seniors in high school. It is not uncommon for a church computer lab to be used in the mornings by elderly people learning to e-mail their grandchildren and in the evenings by a youth group playing Bible software games. In one church's computer lab, the youth group serves as teachers and the senior citizens as students. While worship issues often divide churches along generational lines, many congregations find that computer technology bridges these generational divides. For example, one synagogue runs a genealogy workshop for seniors in their lab. Younger members teach them about various computer technologies—from word processing to scanning pictures—in order to assemble their family genealogies.

Parishes and churches that run parochial schools work hard at using computer labs. One large Catholic parish in Indianapolis is designing a new library featuring a computer lab to serve both parish and school. The church envisions it as a place where young and old, parishioner and student, are engaged in the common task of growing in knowledge and in faith.

PROPHETIC STATEMENT 7:
YOU WILL WORSHIP AND EDUCATE

We also predict increasing use of multimedia presentations for worship and education. This is the glitziest application of computer technology and is one that even very traditional congregations are using. Software such as PowerPoint, coupled with projectors or large-screen televisions and DVD players, are being used to replace worship bulletins, provide visual sermon outlines, display songs and music, and show illustrative video clips. This exciting and up-to-date technology means the end of outdated pull-down maps in Sunday school classes. These new images, as current as the latest archeological finds, mean Bible students can trace Paul's missionary journeys or follow the Israelites' exodus route. Classrooms of children can take part in an interactive encounter in Noah's Ark, face down lions with Daniel, or take part in a host of other games that enhance biblical literacy. As one church in Indianapolis advertises, "This is not the church you grew up in."

Again, you need to be motivated to use this technology not by its entertainment value but by its strategic effectiveness as it relates to your mission. One very traditional Baptist church in Indianapolis, for instance, decided that it was not successfully bringing the message of Christ to younger people. Its worship practices needed to change. The church's decision to use multimedia technology in a new alternative worship service was driven not by the desire to appear relevant or current with the times, but "to find the most effective ways of communicating the gospel." "Using these technologies was one way to do that," the pastor explained.

Though some of the splashier and more publicized experiments of the "wired church" attract the most attention and concern, that does not need to be the case. Focus on using computer technology to make the ministries you are already engaged in more effective, attractive, and applicable to the lives of the people you serve. This is especially true for the young people of your congregation. For them, these technologies are as familiar a part of everyday life as using the telephone—a cell phone, that is.

Whether or not your congregation will or should use computer technology is not the question. The question is *how* your congregation can best use these technologies to enhance your community and mission.

PROPHETIC STATEMENT 8:
YOU WILL TRAIN AND REVISIT YOUR PLAN

We also predict that the congregations best prepared for the wise use of technology will do two additional things. First, they won't undervalue training and technical support. Training and support are worth every dollar spent.

Second, a wise congregation will revisit its technology needs on a regular basis and update software and hardware in a timely manner. What's a timely manner? Well, that is up to you and your congregational culture.

We are not saying that you need to replace something (hardware or software) just because something new comes along. In some ways, the old saw, "If it ain't broke, don't fix it" applies. If your software and hardware is doing what you need and want, then there may be no need to upgrade. Even if your software and hardware are working fine for you, however, you still need to know what upgrades and improvements are offered. That way you can decide if you need them or not. Otherwise it may be too late. At your next upgrade—or users meeting—you will find that you are using a set of expensive doorstops that do not do what you want or need.

PROPHETIC STATEMENT 9:
YOU WILL FIND THAT VON NEUMANN WAS RIGHT

Our final prediction is that John Von Neumann, a brilliant mathematician and consultant to IBM for advanced technology projects, was right in 1949. That's when he said, "It would appear that we have reached the limits of what it is possible to achieve with computer technology, although one should be careful with such statements, as they tend to sound pretty silly in five years." Amen.

Appendix A

TECHNOLOGY ASSESSMENT FORM

Telephony

Do you have more than one phone line?
☐ Yes   ☐ No   ☐ Don't Know

Are you using Centrex?
☐ Yes   ☐ No   ☐ Don't Know

Do you have a phone tree?
☐ Yes   ☐ No   ☐ Don't Know

Do you have a phone system with a central control unit?
☐ Yes   ☐ No   ☐ Don't Know

Do you have voicemail?
☐ Yes   ☐ No   ☐ Don't Know

Do you have an answering machine?
☐ Yes   ☐ No   ☐ Don't Know

Other Office Equipment

Do you have a copier?
    ☐ Yes   ☐ No   ☐ Don't Know

Do you have a fax machine?
    ☐ Yes   ☐ No   ☐ Don't Know

Do you have typewriters?
    ☐ Yes   ☐ No   ☐ Don't Know

If yes, how many?
    ☐ 1   ☐ 2–4 ☐ 5+ ☐ Don't Know

Do you have a mimeograph or duplicating machine?
    ☐ Yes   ☐ No   ☐ Don't Know

Do you have a postage meter?
    ☐ Yes   ☐ No   ☐ Don't Know

Do you have a stand-alone word processor?
    ☐ Yes   ☐ No   ☐ Don't Know

Do you have a label maker?
    ☐ Yes   ☐ No   ☐ Don't Know

Do you have dictation equipment?
    ☐ Yes   ☐ No   ☐ Don't Know

Do you have cable or closed-circuit TV?
    ☐ Yes   ☐ No   ☐ Don't Know

Do you have other types of office equipment?
    ☐ Yes (If yes, please list)   ☐ No   ☐ Don't Know

Computer

Do you have any existing computers?
☐ Yes   ☐ No (If no, skip this section)

Total number of computers
☐ 1   ☐ 2–4 ☐ 5+ ☐ Don't Know

Number of computers older than two years
☐ 1   ☐ 2–4 ☐ 5+ ☐ Don't Know

Are you using a word-processing program?
☐ Yes   ☐ No

If yes, which one?
☐ MS Word   ☐ AmiPro   ☐ WordPerfect
☐ Works   ☐ Other   ☐ Don't Know

Are you using a spreadsheet program?
☐ Yes   ☐ No

If yes, which one?
☐ Excel   ☐ Lotus   ☐ Quattro Pro
☐ Works   ☐ Other   ☐ Don't Know

Are you using any kind of database?
☐ Yes   ☐ No

If yes, which one?
☐ Access   ☐ Dbase   ☐ Clipper
☐ Other   ☐ Don't Know

Are you using your computer(s) for any one of the following?
☐ Accounting   ☐ Calendar   ☐ Presentations
☐ Education   ☐ E-mail   ☐ Scanning
☐ Music

Are your computers networked?
  ☐ Yes   ☐ No   ☐ Don't Know

If yes, what are you using?
  ☐ Novell   ☐ Lantastic   ☐ Windows NT
  ☐ Other   ☐ Don't Know

Do you have any Macintosh computers?
  ☐ Yes   ☐ No   ☐ Don't Know

If yes, how many?
  ☐ 1   ☐ 2–4   ☐ 5+   ☐ Don't Know

Do any of your computers have modems?
  ☐ Yes   ☐ No   ☐ Don't Know

Do you have any printers?
  ☐ Yes   ☐ No   ☐ Don't Know

If yes, what type(s)?
  ☐ Dot Matrix   ☐ Laser   ☐ Inkjet or Bubblejet
  ☐ Daisywheel   ☐ Don't Know

Appendix B

CONGREGATIONAL CULTURE QUESTIONS

The following questions will help you answer some of your congregation's most important culture questions related to choosing a CMS package. These questions are not a features checklist; rather, they are a tool to help you think about the practices and customs of your congregation. Your responses will help you pick the CMS that is right for your congregation.

- ☐ Do you use numbered offering envelopes?
- ☐ Do couples/families share a common envelope number?
- ☐ Does a person/couple/family keep the same envelope number from year to year?
- ☐ Do you record contributions of nonmembers?
- ☐ Do you take pledges to church funds?
- ☐ Are any of these pledges multiyear?
- ☐ Is your pledge year the same as a calendar year?
- ☐ Is your financial year the same as a calendar year?
- ☐ Are your contribution records kept on a computer at the church or at another location?
- ☐ Do pastors and/or other staff have access to contribution information? Do they need to?
- ☐ How often do you want to send contribution statements to the congregation?
- ☐ How often do you write checks?
- ☐ Do you use computer-generated checks?

☐ Do you want to process payroll for employees or to use a payroll service?

☐ Do you use a cash or accrual method of accounting?

☐ Is the person who manages your day-to-day financial transactions an accountant, or do they have other accounting experience?

☐ Do some couples in the same family wish to have both first names on labels and other correspondence (e.g., John and Mary Smith versus Mr. and Mrs. John Smith)?

☐ Do some couples with different last names wish to have both last names on labels and other correspondence (e.g., John Smith and Mary Miller)?

☐ Do members of the same family sometimes have different addresses?

☐ What individual date information is important to your congregation (e.g., marriage, baptism, profession of faith)?

☐ Is e-mail used for regular correspondence with the congregation? Individually and groups?

☐ Do you use a Phonetree or other automated voice system to send voice messages to the congregation?

☐ Do you send personalized correspondence to large numbers of people in the congregation?

☐ Do you print individual addresses directly on envelopes or do you use labels all of the time?

☐ Is bulk-mail sorting used for any communication to the congregation?

☐ When a person dies or leaves the congregation, do you still want to keep information about them (e.g., family connections, address, contribution or attendance information)?

☐ Is it important to record the date when a person dies or leaves?

☐ What are the special areas of ministry in your congregation that you would like to track in a computer database?

☐ Can the person in charge of your membership data make decisions about the design of the database (more powerful), or should the software provide all of the structure (less chance for error)?

☐ Do you want to know who has (or has not) attended worship, church school classes, or other events?

☐ Do you want to keep track of attendance with both members and visitors?

☐ Do you want to know who takes communion during a worship service?

☐ Do you have multiple weekly worship services?

☐ Do you follow up with members who have missed several consecutive worship services, classes, and other events?

☐ Do you want that information to be kept in a computer database?

☐ Do you have several levels of organization for church school or other classes, and do you wish to use them in reporting (e.g., area, department, age, class name)?

☐ Do you use the Internet to publish membership, contribution, or financial information?

Appendix C

WHAT DO YOU *WANT* TO DO THAT A CMS *CAN* DO?

☐ Keep track of people with different kinds of relationships to your congregation (members, visitors, constituents, children and spouse of members, etc.).

☐ Use different kinds of telephone numbers—fax, cell, pager, etc.

☐ Distinguish which numbers are published or unpublished.

☐ Have more than one address for a family, and have individual addresses for family members.

☐ Keep e-mail information and use e-mail to communicate with members individually or as a group.

☐ Track life events for individuals and families.

☐ Track skills and talents.

☐ Track ministry service, leadership roles, and small-group activities—which may have start and end dates.

☐ Keep information of spiritual gifts identified and used. Follow a spiritual gifts identification process.

☐ Keep digital photos of individuals and/or families.

☐ Print church directories with or without photos.

☐ Print labels for correspondence.

☐ Use mail merge for personalized communications to congregation.

☐ Use searches to define groups of people who meet certain criteria (e.g., all married men who live in one zip code for a targeted mailing) and save searches which will be frequently used.

☐ Allow individuals and families to choose their own label names and salutations.

☐ Retain information about people who die or leave the congregation, but prevent them from showing up on lists, reports, and directories.

☐ Allow different family members to have different last names.

☐ Add "people" information by importing data from another database—by yourself.

☐ Export information to other software—Access, Excel, Word, etc.

☐ Keep attendance information about any or all people in the database.

☐ Keep attendance for worship, communion, church school, classes, or other events.

☐ Keep attendance for more than one kind of worship service, and have the ability to group services together.

☐ Identify persons who have been absent from church events and print reports to use in follow-up.

☐ Promote church school or other classes as a group.

☐ Print class rosters and attendance marking sheets.

☐ Print numerical attendance summaries for classes or worship.

☐ View or print attendance information about one person over a long period.

☐ Keep attendance information detail for more than one year.

☐ Use bar coding to record attendance.

☐ Do contribution entry onsite or from a remote location.

☐ Keep contribution information to more than one church fund (operating, building, mission, etc.).

☐ Track pledges to a fund, and credit contributions against a pledge. Have the ability to track multiyear pledges.

☐ Print contribution statements annually, quarterly, monthly, etc.

☐ Use a customized contribution statement format.

☐ Use mail merge containing contribution information.

☐ Enter contributions by name or envelope number.

☐ Allow contributors to have individual or joint envelope numbers, pledges, and giving records.

☐ Record check numbers for individual contributions.

☐ Use a check scanner to automate contribution entry.

☐ Use pledge or contribution information in data searches for labels, directories, or other reports.

☐ Print contribution and/or pledge reports for different funds.

☐ Keep detailed contribution information for more than one year at a time.

☐ Automatically assign envelope numbers.

☐ Export reports to word processing or spreadsheet software.

☐ E-mail contribution reports or statements to givers.

☐ Model a formal congregation visitation program. Assign volunteers to make visits, record visit notes, categorize visits by type, follow-up visits with other types of communication.

☐ Model a formal volunteer program and process. Help members discover their gifts and talents. Assign steps to the volunteering process. Record notes from interviews of potential volunteers. Keep track of volunteer opportunities, and match potential volunteers with those opportunities by skill and availability.

☐ Maintain a reservation system for congregational events. Record the names and payment information of people who are registered for an event. Produce event reports.

☐ Keep money in more than one bank account, or separate funds in the same bank account.

☐ Track actual income and expenses by account.

☐ Use budgets for each account—vary by month based upon history, percentage assignment, or manual entry.

☐ Have true fund accounting—keep track of several different congregational funds, such as operating, mission, building, memorials, etc.

☐ Create your own account number formats—numeric, alpha, and character.

☐ Have major and minor account groupings (e.g., area, department).

☐ Do financial project tracking across groupings.

☐ Print balance sheets, statements of revenue and expenses, detailed journals—on demand.

☐ Maintain vendor information files.

☐ Enter vendor invoices—detail by account, combining all entries for one vendor.

☐ Use cash or accrual accounting methods.

☐ Reconcile bank statements.

☐ Print computer checks.

☐ Customize standard accounting reports—add, delete, change columns.

☐ Export budget and accounting information to a spreadsheet.

☐ Import budget information from a spreadsheet.

☐ Have online inquiry, MTD, YTD, all years by vendor, and account.

☐ Pay employees.

☐ Automatically do tax calculations for employee payroll.

☐ Take care of special tax circumstance for clergy— FICA, Medicare, and housing allowance.

☐ Account for deductions for insurance, extra tax, savings plan, etc.

☐ Automatically calculate local taxes.

☐ Direct deposit to one or more bank accounts.

☐ Keep an employee information file.

☐ Allow for variable pay periods and salary—monthly, semimonthly, biweekly, weekly, hourly.

☐ Have more than one overtime rate.

☐ Have vacation holiday and sick time accrual, deductions, and calculations.

☐ Payroll check printing, gross pay, deductions to net.

☐ Tax reporting—W-2, 1099, Form 941, Federal summaries, state, and local reporting.

☐ Print payroll reports by individual, time period, account number.

☐ Keep inventory of assets—quantity, location, value, and description.

☐ Automatically calculate asset depreciation— alternate methods—and summarize.

☐ Schedule rooms for specific calendar events, internal or external.

☐ Schedule equipment and vehicles for specific events.

☐ Record and print room set-up information with room schedules for building staff.

☐ Print schedule and calendar reports for congregational and staff use.

☐ Receive income from a business or operation other than member contributions, such as a congregational bookstore or preschool.

☐ Maintain student, family, and tuition records for a congregational school, preschool, or daycare.
☐ Use on an individual computer.
☐ Use on a network with multiple workstations.
☐ Use from a remote location (not in the physical facility).
☐ Have access via the Internet.

Appendix D

THINGS YOU CAN DO

Administration

Already Doing	Want to Do	Don't Know or N/A	
☐	☐	☐	Do you write letters?
☐	☐	☐	Do you write form letters?
☐	☐	☐	Do you do mailings (address labels)?
☐	☐	☐	Do you address envelopes?
☐	☐	☐	Do you keep a calendar for church events?
☐	☐	☐	Do you create, use, and distribute church directories?
☐	☐	☐	Do you keep track of the birthdays and anniversaries of members?
☐	☐	☐	Do you keep track of information about your members?
☐	☐	☐	Do you keep track of contributions?
☐	☐	☐	Do you keep track of attendance?
☐	☐	☐	Do you gather and keep information about people who visit your church?
☐	☐	☐	Do you report church giving to missions or other outside organizations?
☐	☐	☐	Do you report information to a denomination?
☐	☐	☐	Do you do bulk mailings?

Administration (cont.)

Already Doing	Want to Do	Don't Know or N/A	
☐	☐	☐	Do you report financial information to church groups?
☐	☐	☐	Do you track volunteers' skills/interests/participation?
☐	☐	☐	Do you schedule facilities for outside activities?
☐	☐	☐	Do you keep track of individual staff appointments?
☐	☐	☐	Does your staff communicate with
☐	☐	☐	staff of other congregations?
☐	☐	☐	Do you schedule A/V equipment?
☐	☐	☐	Do you make copies?
			Do you have a Web site?
			Do you keep track of visits by
☐	☐	☐	staff or volunteers (e.g., hospital,
☐	☐	☐	birth, death, etc.)?
			Do you have a prayer network?
☐	☐	☐	Do you have an organized system of congregational care?
☐	☐	☐	Do you purchase supplies or materials by mail order?
			Do you have any recurring mainte-
☐	☐	☐	nance (piano tuning, furnace filters, vehicle oil change, etc.)?
☐	☐	☐	Do you provide resources to persons in need?
			Do you keep an inventory of
☐	☐	☐	equipment, furnishings, and/or supplies?
☐	☐	☐	Do you have files of historical documents?

Communication

Already Doing	Want to Do	Don't Know or N/A	
☐	☐	☐	Do you keep old newsletters and bulletins?
☐	☐	☐	
☐	☐	☐	Do you create and distribute congregational newsletters?
☐	☐	☐	Do you make your own flyers, signs, or brochures?
☐	☐	☐	Do you communicate with other churches?
☐	☐	☐	Do you communicate with denominational offices?
☐	☐	☐	Do you search for educational resources (use outside resources)?
☐	☐	☐	Do you print or publish sermons?
☐	☐	☐	Do you look at other church and/or denominational Web sites?
☐	☐	☐	Do you use recorded music?
			Do you have church dinners and other fellowship events?
☐	☐	☐	Do you track life-cycle events (birth, marriage, divorce, baptism, bris/namings, bar/bat mitzvah, death)?
			Do you advertise worship services or other congregational events?

Education

Already Doing	Want to Do	Don't Know or N/A	
☐	☐	☐	
☐	☐	☐	Do you have libraries with books, music, and/or resources?
☐	☐	☐	Do you print and create educational materials (religious schools)?
☐	☐	☐	Do you keep track of educational participation?

Education (cont.)

Already Doing	Want to Do	Don't Know or N/A	
☐	☐	☐	Do you use educational tools (maps, atlases, etc.)?
☐	☐	☐	Do you schedule staff?

Worship

Already Doing	Want to Do	Don't Know or N/A	
☐	☐	☐	Do you communicate with other educational institutions?
☐	☐	☐	Do you print your own songbooks?
☐	☐	☐	Do you make your own worship folders or devotional booklets/inserts?
☐	☐	☐	Do you print bulletins for worship services?
☐	☐	☐	Do you use photographs or drawings in printed material?
☐	☐	☐	Do you create or transpose music?

Appendix E: Sample Technology Plan budget

PRIORITY	ITEM	QUANTITY	COST EACH	TOTAL COST	VENDOR	NOTES	PERSON RESPONSIBLE
High	**Network Server**						
	PowerEdge 660 server w/ Xeon 2.0 GHz processor	1	6,499.00	6,499.00	Dell	Free shipping thru July 3-yr onsite warranty, parts and labor	Mary
	4 GB DDR SDRAM						
	4—36 GB SCSI hard drives						
	PowerVault 110T tape backup						
	Floppy/CD-Rom drives						
	15" digital flat-screen monitor						
	Mouse, keyboard						
High	**Server Software**						
	Windows Server 2003 Standard w/ 10 client licenses	1	325.00	325.00	Softchoice	Microsoft Charity Open License	Mary
	Microsoft Exchange 2003 w/ 10 client licenses	1	750.00	750.00	Softchoice	Microsoft Charity Open License	Mary
	Norton AntiVirus Corporate Edition w/ 10 client licenses	1	227.00	227.00	PC Mall		Mary
High	**Network Cabling - wire drops**	10	125.00	1,250.00	Joe's Cable Shop		Eric
High	**Network Hardware**						
	24-Port 1GHz switch	1	199.00	199.00	Computer Warehouse		Eric
	DSL router	1	486.00	486.00	Computer Warehouse		Eric
	Wall-mounted rack	1	157.00	157.00	Computer Warehouse		Eric
	Patch cable board—24 port	1	99.00	99.00	Computer Warehouse		Eric
	Cat 5 cables—3'	25	2.07	51.75	Joe's Cable Shop		Eric
	Cat 5 cables—10'	15	5.86	87.90	Joe's Cable Shop		Eric
	DLT 4000/7000 backup tape media	5	33.00	165.00	Dell		Mary
Medium	**Desktop Computers**						
	Pentium 4 3.2 GHz	3	1,500.00	4,500.00	Dell	Will purchase in third quarter recheck price and specs	Mary
	1 GB SDRAM						
	2 USB ports						
	80 GB Hard Drive						
	Integrated network capability						
	Intellimouse, keyboard						
	17" digital flat-screen monitor						
Medium	**Software for Desktops**						
	MS Windows XP Professional	3	27.00	81.00	Softchoice	MS Charity Open License	Mary
	MS Office XP Professional	3	89.00	267.00	Softchoice	MS Charity Open License for Pastor Susan	Mary
	BibleWorks software	1	350.00	350.00	Christian Publishing		Mary
Low	**Digital Camera**						
	Canon Digital Rebel SLR w/ 18-55 zoom lens	1	900.00	900.00	Roberts	Possible next year purchase Eric recheck price and specs	
	TOTAL TECHNOLOGY PLAN COST			**$16,394.65**			

129

Appendix F
CREATING A TECHNOLOGY PLAN: SUMMARY

A technology plan is a blueprint for implementing short-, medium-, and long-range technology of a congregation. Here's the process we suggest to create a technology plan:

1. Create a technology team that includes "stakeholders." This team needs to have someone representing the pastoral staff, the office staff, the education staff, the financial board or committee, and so on. This committee approach is essential in the successful implementation of a technology plan.
2. Get professional help. There are individuals and companies who can assess your current usage and then make recommendations about how to implement, suggest vendors for both hardware and software, and manage the project. Professional help, used wisely and judiciously, will save money. It also keeps you from making mistakes.
3. Include more training than you think you will need. Make sure staff and volunteers have adequate access to initial and ongoing training.
4. Talk with other congregations. Find out how successful they are at using hardware, software, consultants, training sites—anything you can think of. Be sure to talk with more than one person—

often the pastor's perspective is much different than the administrator's.

5. Don't worry about technology advancing past you. It will. But any hardware and software will still be working for you three to five years from now. Some upgrading will be necessary along the way, especially with software.

6. Get all your records on computer and back up your data. If you have a systematic program for backing up data, you'll be back in business after a system crash in a matter of hours, rather than days.

7. Grow your technology with your needs. Don't buy things you don't need today or in the next six months. Compatibility is not the issue it once was, and most hardware and software integrate easily.

Appendix G

SAMPLE CHURCH: TECHNOLOGY
ACCEPTABLE USE POLICY

This document is meant to be a sample policy for use as a benchmark for congregations to create their own policies and procedures. It does not imply any endorsement, sanction, or authorization from the Indianapolis Center for Congregations or the Alban Institute on such policies.

Technology resources (Internet, e-mail, phone, copier/printers, postal meter, computer, software, etc.) are provided as tools to help our church accomplish its mission. As a Christian church, we expect the staff, volunteers, and other users of the technology services of [Sample Church] to use them in an appropriate manner.

The intent of this policy is not to micromanage your technology usage. There are times when it is acceptable to use the technology for personal reasons. Use your discretion and common sense in determining what is acceptable use and what is not. This determination is subjective—what are considered areas of obvious abuse will be addressed.

Privacy

- Internet/E-mail Usage
  —Each Web page accessed leaves an entry by username and can be tracked.

—All electronic and telephonic communications systems, communications, and information transmitted by and received from, or stored in, these systems are the property of [Sample Church].

- The Information Technology Ministry Team Leader or technical support system may look at your e-mail and stored files but will only do so when there is an administrative need (i.e., virus outbreak).

Stewardship of Resources

- Users should protect their login name and password. You are responsible for anything done under these codes. Changes to passwords need to be reported to the Information Technology Ministry Team Leader.
- Software
  —Do not download or install anything without contacting the Pastor or Information Technology Ministry Team Leader—willful violations could reflect poorly on your employment record.
  —All computer software is purchased and delivered through our technical support vendor or the Information Technology Ministry Team. This allows us to be assured that registration and inventory requirements can be completed.
  —[Sample Church] respects computer software copyrights and adheres to the terms and conditions of all software licenses to which [Sample Church] is a party.
  —Employees may not add, delete, or duplicate software or related documentation for use either on [Sample Church] premises or elsewhere

unless expressly authorized to do so by the Pastor or Information Technology Ministry Team Leader.

—Any software installed on user machines by the users becomes the legal responsibility of the user, and any violations that are subject to legal action become the user's legal responsibility.

—Software may not be installed on home machines without approval of the Pastor or Information Technology Ministry Team.

—Even though the church has virus protection software on each PC, watch for viruses! Do not open file attachments to e-mails if you are not triple sure what they are. If you are not expecting an attachment from someone, confirm with that person that they meant to send it to you before you open it.

- Hardware

—Remember that all technology equipment belongs to [Sample Church] for church purposes and abuse may be addressed.

Usage of Technology

- Be aware that every file you save on the network data drive takes up space on our server.

  —You should periodically delete old files that will not be used again.

  —If you have large amounts of data that you want archived, see the tech support people on their weekly visit or contact the Information Technology Ministry Team Leader. They will show you how to archive your data on a CD-ROM.

- Regularly delete e-mail messages you no longer need.
- Use good judgment on Internet usage; abuse will be addressed.
- Be aware that when you send or receive large e-mail attachments, storage space is taken up. Please remove these files from the Sent Items box and/or the Inbox as soon as they are not needed.

Portable Equipment

The church has a laptop computer and a portable LCD projector. Those items will be under the control of a designated staff member. It is that person's responsibility to track the where-abouts of the equipment. A sign-out and sign-in system will be used to track the equipment. The congregation will be made aware of how to request the use of these resources.

Backup of Data

Each night the system will back up the data from the server to a tape. To ensure the integrity of our backup system, a desig-nated staff member will take the previous days' tape home each night and return it the next day. This allows for keeping a tape offsite in case of a catastrophic event.

I have read, understand, and agree to the terms of this Technology Use Policy.

Signed: _____ Date: _____

Name (printed): _____

Glossary

ADSL (asymmetric digital subscriber line)—a DSL line where the upload speed is different than from the download speed, with the download speed usually faster.

Applet—A Java program embedded in an HTML page.

application—a program designed for a certain purpose; e.g., Microsoft Word is a word-processing application.

attachment—the e-mail version of stapling something to a document. Pictures, audio files, really bad jokes, and viruses are the most common attachments.

bandwidth—usually measured in bits per second. What it means is how much stuff you can send over an Internet connection, which is usually measured in bits per second. The more bandwidth you have, the better.

baud—a modem term that says how many bits a modem can send or receive per second. The higher the number, the faster the modem.

BIOS (basic input/output system)—a program preinstalled on Windows-based computers (not on Macs) that the computer uses to start up. The CPU (central processing unit) accesses the BIOS while booting. Next, BIOS then checks all hardware connections and locates the devices. If everything's okay, BIOS loads the operating system.

bit (**b**inary dig**it**)—the smallest unit of computerized data. Every bit is either an 1 or an 0.

bitmap—a map of bits that looks like a picture. Common bitmap (also known as graphic or clip art) files include BMP, JPEG, GIF, PICT, and TIFF.

blog (We**b log**)—a journaling format that people post on the Web.

boot—what you do when you start your computer. Rebooting is what you do if you restart when it's already running, but crashes.

browser—software that you use to look at Web pages. The two most commonly used are Netscape Navigator and Internet Explorer.

bug—a software design mistake. Really bad bugs can cause your computer to crash.

burner—a device that uses special CDs (CD-R or CD-R+RW) to make copies of CDs and to back up data.

byte—a set of bits representing a single character. There are generally eight bits in a byte.

cable modem—serves the same purpose as a dial-up modem, but is faster.

cache—pronounced "cash." Cache memory is the fastest type of RAM available and is used in CPUs, hard drives, and a variety of other components. The more cache, the better.

CD-ROM (compact disk–read-only memory)—is a tiny 4.72-inch silver disk holding lots of music or other information, but is not recordable or rewritable.

CD-R (compact disk–recordable)—is just like a CD except you can record stuff on it—once!

CD-RW (compact disk–rewritable)—is just like a CD-R except that it can be rewritten many times.

chat—is to e-mail what a conference call is to a regular telephone call. You do it instantaneously and can involve a lot of people at the same time.

client—software that contacts and gets data from a server software program on another computer.

configuration—refers to the technical specifications of a computer, including processor speed, the amount of RAM, hard-drive space, and the type of video card.

cookie—information sent by a Web server to a Web browser which the browser saves and sends back to the server whenever the browser makes additional requests from the server. Clear as mud, right? It's used for things such as login or registration information, online "shopping cart" information, user preferences, and so forth.

CPU (central processing unit)—the part of the computer that computes. It's also known as the "processor."

crash—when the computer suddenly freezes, locks up, or generally stops working.

database—software that organizes information, typically in linked tables of rows and columns in such a way that the data can be easily searched, sorted, and updated. Popular database software includes Microsoft Access and FileMaker Pro.

default—used to describe a preset value for some option in a computer program, such as font type and size. Many times default settings are what most people would choose anyway, but you can usually change them if you want.

desktop—the main working area of your computer, where all the program icons are.

desktop publisher—software for creating bulletins, posters, newsletters, flyers, business cards, and so on.

dial in (or dial up)—a way of connecting to the Internet via a regular phone line or a terminal adapter to connect via an ISDN phone line.

digital camera—looks and works like a regular camera, but instead of film, it stores images as a file made up of bits and bytes.

directory—can be also called a "folder." It's a collection of files usually grouped together for organizational purposes.

disk—used for storing data that doesn't forget the data when there's no power. Some disks are removable (e.g., floppy disks, Zip disks); others are not (e.g., hard disks).

domain name—the unique name that identifies an Internet site (e.g., centerforcongregations.org). Domain names always have two or more parts, separated by dots. The left side (centerforcongregations) is the most specific and the right (org) is general.

download—what you do when transferring data from another computer to the computer you are using. The opposite is *upload*.

drive—a device for storing or retrieving data (see *disk* above).

driver—what your computer uses to talk to hardware devices. It is a small file that holds all the information the computer needs to recognize and control the device.

DSL (digital subscriber line)—a way of moving data over regular phone lines, configured to connect two specific locations, and that is faster than a regular phone connection.

DVD—means "digital versatile disc" or "digital video disc." A DVD looks like a CD, but can store, in computer terms, a whole bunch more stuff.

e-mail (electronic mail)—are messages sent via computer instead of the U.S. Postal Service. E-mail can also be sent automatically to a large number of addresses.

ethernet—a very common method of networking computers in a local area network.

extranet—an intranet accessible to computers that are not physically part of a congregation's private network, but that is not accessible to the general public (e.g., to allow denominational officials or other partners access to your Web site).

file—a unit of named information stored on a computer.

file compression—is used to reduce the size computer files for uploading and downloading, which speeds file-transfer time. PKZip is one software package used for doing this.

firewall—a combination of hardware and software that separates a network for security purposes.

folder—the cyber version of the manila file folder you store things in. It holds and organizes documents, applications, and other computer files.

format—allows information to be recognized by your computer, especially software. Different software uses different formats for word processing, spreadsheets, publishing, and so on.

FTP (file transfer protocol)—one way of moving files between two Internet sites.

gigabyte—either 1000 or 1024 megabytes, depending on who's measuring.

GPU (graphics processing unit)—a single-chip processor and is similar to the CPU. Used primarily for things such as lighting effects and three-dimensional motion.

GUI (graphical user interface)—refers to the graphical interface of a computer which allows users to click and drag objects with a mouse. Windows and Mac OS are both GUI-based. Pronounced "goo-ey."

hard drive—where most of the data, including files and folders, in your computer is stored. It spins really fast so that data can be accessed immediately from where it's stored magnetically on the drive.

hardware—the stuff you can touch. The keyboard, monitor, mouse, scanner, printer, tower, speakers, and so forth.

hit—used to mean a single request from a browser for a single item from a server. That means if you look at a page that has three pictures and one piece of text, you've made four hits.

home page (or homepage)—the main page for a Web site.

host—any computer on a network that serves as a repository for services (e.g., e-mail, Web site) available to other computers networked to it.

HTML (hypertext markup language)—the language used to make hypertext documents for the Web. It's similar to old-fashioned typesetting code in that you surround a text with codes that say how it should look.

HTTP (hypertext transfer protocol)—how hypertext files move across the Internet.

hub—hardware used to network multiple computers together, usually ethernet-based, allowing information sent to the hub to flow to any other computer on the network.

hypertext—any Web text that contains links to other documents (usually words or phrases that, if chosen, open another Internet document or site).

icon—a fundamental feature of GUI and makes computing more user-friendly than having to enter text commands to do anything. By clicking and dragging icons, you can move the actual files they represent to various locations on your computer's hard drive, and by double-clicking an application icon you can open the program. Macintosh introduced icons in 1984.

Internet (lowercase *i*)—any time you connect two or more networks together.

Internet (uppercase *I*)—that huge collection of interconnected networks connected using the TCP/IP protocols. Also known as the World Wide Web.

intranet—a private network that uses the same kinds of software found on the Internet, but that is only for internal use.

ISDN (integrated services digital network)—a way of moving data over existing regular phone lines. Unlike DSL, ISDN can be used to connect to many different locations, one at a time, just like a regular telephone call, as long the other location also has ISDN.

ISP (Internet service provider)—an organization (such as AOL or AT&T) that provides, usually for a fee, access to the Internet.

Java—a programming language invented by Sun Microsystems. Java creates programs that can be safely downloaded to your computer through the Internet and run without worrying about viruses or other nasty things. Small Java programs, called Applets, in Web pages allow them to include things such as animations, calculators, and other stuff.

kilobyte—a thousand bytes. Well, really, it's 1024 bytes. Approximately.

LAN (local area network)—a computer network usually located all in the same facility or office, hence "local."

login—the account name used to access a computer system (not secret, unlike a password) or the act of connecting to a computer system by giving your "user name" and "password."

mail list (or mailing list)—is a system that allows people to send e-mail to one address and have it automatically copied and sent to all the subscribers to that mail list.

megabyte—a million bytes. (Okay, so it's really 1024 kilobytes.)

microprocessor—a little chip that's the brains of a computer. It does all the adding, subtracting, multiplying, and dividing that a computer does to work.

MIDI (musical instrument digital interface)—the standard that musicians use to hook together keyboards, synthesizers, and other musical instruments and computer equipment, allowing them to create and edit digital music tracks.

modem (**MO**dulator, **DEM**odulator)—a telephone for a computer, allowing one computer to talk to another over phone lines.

motherboard—the main circuit board of your computer, holding CPU, ROM, memory expansion slots, PCI slots, serial ports, USB ports, and controllers for things such as the hard drive, DVD drive, keyboard, and mouse. Basically, the motherboard is what makes everything in your computer work together.

MP3 (MPEG-1 audio layer-3)—the most popular compressed audio file format, which is about one-tenth the size of the original audio file while remaining nearly CD-quality.

MPEG (moving picture experts group)—a compressed movie file that can contain both audio and video while maintaining most of the original quality.

multimedia—the integration of multiple media, including text, graphics, audio, video, and so forth. CDs and DVDs are often considered to be "multimedia."

network—whenever you connect two or more computers together so that they can share resources.

OCR (optical character recognition)—allows you to scan that paper you lost on your hard drive, but fortunately printed out, back into your computer. An OCR program converts the characters on the page into a text document that can be read by a word-processing program.

office suite—a set of software that includes, at minimum, a word-processing, spreadsheet, and database program.

operating system (OS)—the software that communicates with computer hardware on the most basic level. It allocates memory, processes tasks, accesses disks, and peripherials, and serves as the user interface. Without an operating system, no software will run.

parallel port—a 25-pin interface found on the back of a computer that is used for connecting external devices such as a printer or a scanner. USB is replacing this on many computers.

password—a code used to login to a system. Good passwords have letters, numbers, and symbols and are not simple like "7deadlysins."

PDA (personal digital assistant)—a little electronic device that takes notes, keeps dates, tracks appointments, sorts phone numbers, sends e-mail, edits documents, and lets you read publications like *USA Today*. And it can "sync" this information with your computer.

PDF (portable document format)—Adobe Systems' way of capturing text, images, and formatting of documents from a variety of applications. PDF documents come across the Internet looking the same way on your screen as they did when originally created. To view PDF files, you need Adobe Acrobat Reader, distributed free by Adobe.

pixel (short for "picture element")—one of the little dots that make up the images on computer displays. Each pixel is just one color at a time, but because they're so small, they appear to blend to form various shades and blends of colors.

port—(1) the place where information goes in or out (or both) of a computer, such as the serial port; (2) on the Internet, refers to a number that is part of a URL, appearing after a colon (:) right after the domain name; (3) translating a piece of software so that it will run on another type of computer (e.g., to translate a Windows program so that is will run on a Macintosh).

portal—a Web site that is meant to be the first place a user goes when using the Internet. It usually has a catalog of Web sites, a search engine, and offers e-mail and other services to get people to use it as their main portal to the Web.

RAM (random-access memory)—made up of small memory chips connected to your motherboard. When you open a program, it loads from the hard drive into the RAM because it reads faster that way. The more RAM you have, the more data can be loaded from the hard drive into the RAM, which can help speed up your computer.

registry—the database used by Microsoft Windows to store configuration information about the software installed on a computer, including the desktop background, program settings, and file extension associations. Whenever you install a program, it will usually write some data to the computer's registry. Don't edit the registry unless you really know what you're doing. (If you want to know why, see *crash.*)

ROM (read-only memory)—not to be confused with *RAM.* ROM contains hardwired instructions that the computer uses when it boots up, before the system software loads.

router—a special-purpose computer or software package that handles the connection between two or more packet-switched networks. Routers spend all their time looking at the source and destination addresses of the packets passing through them and deciding which route to send them on.

scanner—a piece of hardware that takes a picture of a picture (or document) and produces a computer file that represents what has been scanned.

scrolling—how you move through a document that is too big to see on the monitor at one time. You use the scroll bars in the application or move the mouse to scroll up and down, side to side.

SDSL (symmetric digital subscriber line)—a type of DSL where upload and download speeds are the same.

search engine—most known as a Web-based system for searching information available on the Internet. Yahoo and Google are two commonly used search engines.

server—a computer or piece of software that provides a specific kind of service to client software on other computers. It can refer to a particular piece of software or to the machine on which the software is running.

shortcut—an icon that allows you to open something (e.g., a document, program, and so forth) directly from your desktop.

software—computer programs for word processing, Internet browsing, and so forth.

spam (or spamming)—the same message is sent to a large number of people who didn't ask for it or want it.

spreadsheet—a type of software used to perform various calculations. It is especially popular for financial applications.

streaming—when a multimedia file can be played back without being completely downloaded first. This means you can watch a video or listen to a sound file while it's being downloaded to your computer. Real Audio and QuickTime documents can be streaming files.

T-1—a leased-line connection capable of carrying data at 1,544,000 bits per second and are commonly used to connect large LANs to the Internet.

tape drive—a removable storage device mainly used for backing up data, often to make incremental backups (daily, weekly, monthly, etc.), which is much cheaper than using multiple hard drives.

terabyte—1000 gigabytes.

terminal—a device that allows you to send commands to a computer somewhere else because the software acts like a physical terminal and allows you to type commands to the other computer.

terminal server—a special-purpose computer that has places to plug in many modems on one side, and a connection to a LAN or host machine on the other side. Thus the terminal server does the work of answering the calls and passes the connections on to the appropriate node. Most terminal servers can provide PPP or SLIP services if connected to the Internet.

upload—when you transfer data from the computer you are using to another computer. The opposite of *download*.

URL (uniform resource locator)—an Internet address.

USB (universal serial bus)—a port that can be used to connect a mouse, keyboard, game controllers, printers, scanners, and removable media drives. And it's faster than older ports (serial or parallel ports).

user—a person who uses a computer.

virus—a piece of malicious computer programming code that copies itself . . . over . . . and over . . . and over . . .

VPN (virtual private network)—a network in which some of the parts are connected using the public Internet, but the data is encrypted, so the entire network is "virtually" private.

WAN (wide area network)—a network covering an area larger than a single building or campus.

Web page—a document designed for viewing in a Web browser and is typically written in HTML.

Webmaster—a person in charge of maintaining a Web site.

wi-fi (wireless fidelity)—refers to wireless network components that should be recognized by any wi-fi certified access point, and vice-versa.

word-processing program—software designed to help with the production of text documents like letters and memos.

worm—a virus that does not infect other programs but makes copies of itself and infects additional computers, usually over the Internet.

WWW (World Wide Web)—a term often used (incorrectly) when referring to the Internet: (1) the whole range of resources that can be accessed using Gopher, FTP, HTTP, telnet, USENET, WAIS, among other tools; (2) hypertext servers, commonly called "Web servers," which serve Web pages to Web browsers.

Zip drive—an inexpensive disk drive made by Iomega Systems. It uses removable 100- and 250-megabyte hard disks and is suitable for moving files.

Made in the USA
Lexington, KY
27 June 2018